You'll go to London

Lionel Ball

You'll go to London

The Autobiography of Lionel Ball

Lionel Ball

Unless otherwise indicated Scripture quotations are taken from the *Holy Bible New International Version*. Copyright © 1973, 1978, 1984 by International Bible Society. Used by permission of Hodder & Stoughton Publishers, A member of the Hodder Headline Group. All rights reserved. "NIV" is a registered trademark of International Bible Society. UK trademark number 1448790.

Scripture quotations marked "NKJV" are taken from the *New King James Version*. Copyright © 1982 by Thomas Nelson, Inc. Used by permission. All rights reserved.

Scripture quotations marked KJV are taken from the *King James Version*.

Photo's marked with a † are used with the kind permission of Peter Trainer.

ISBN 978-1-84550-314-7

Copyright © Lionel Ball

10 9 8 7 6 5 4 3 2 1

Published in 2008
by
Christian Focus Publications Ltd.,
Geanies House, Fearn, Ross-shire,
Scotland, UK, IV20 1TW

www.christianfocus.com

Cover design by Daniel Van Straaten

Printed by Norhaven Paperback A/S

Contents

FOREWORD

By Rt. Revd Sandy Millar

When I first met Lionel Ball early in 1971 I little knew what fun we would have together in the years to come or how much I would learn from him and from the workings of the London City Mission.

In those days – before I was married and before I was ordained – I worshipped as a layman at Holy Trinity Brompton. Lionel bravely threw open the Medical Mission Hall in Short's Gardens and a team of us from Holy Trinity Brompton came together to help him Thursday by Thursday.

The world of the back streets, as it seemed to me, congregated on those evenings; the hall full of smoke and the smell of damp, unwashed clothing; faces the same, unshaved as well; often with a dog on the end of a string, teeth in short supply, thankfully, like those of their owners, and each had a particular tale to tell if any-one had the time or inclination to listen.

Lionel presided with his infectious good humour and great musical gifts. He would play and we would all help with the singing as best we could. 'Now I belong to Jesus...' 'What a Friend we have in Jesus', 'The Lord's My Shepherd'. I distinctly remember the look of wistful sadness that often came over some of the older street folk who had wandered in as they struggled to recall words long since forgotten in the challenges and failures in life that had led them to settle for homelessness and the wandering lifestyle to which they had fallen. Some of the younger ones were still not reconciled to a life from which there seemed no escape; their brash demands and constant threats of violence meant that the team spent much of the evening on tenterhooks, constant in prayer and conscious of our total dependence on God to keep us from being swallowed up in rows and brawls not of our own making. And yet, underneath, I think Annette (now my wife) and I always felt that somehow this was where God was.

In the Song of Songs (1:7, 8) the beloved calls out to her lover, *'Tell me, you whom I love, where you graze your flock and where you rest your sheep ...'* and her friends offer her the best advice you can ever be given: *'if you do not know, most beautiful of women, <u>follow the tracks of the sheep and graze your young goats by the tents of the shepherds.</u>'* I used to think that the tracks of the sheep at that time led to Short's Gardens and the Medical Mission Hall. It was there that I first formed a lifelong admiration for the patient work of the London City Mission and through Lionel came to meet some of the missionaries. They seemed to be close to the Lord, able to compensate for the disappointments and in so many ways the manifest unfairness of so much of life with a humour that reached across every sort of potential social barrier – or perhaps it was just Lionel that was like that. Every Thursday night, having tasted of God's love for the poor and with my hair and every article of clothing reeking of that Thursday evening fug, I and the team would return to our day jobs, leaving Lionel to deal with every sort of situation that had come up in conversations all over the hall, to all of which the only suggestion that I could think to make was, "Why don't you have a word with Lionel?"

Along with my increasing admiration for the work of the London City Mission, was growing at that time a, for me, quite new sense of the call of God on my own life. What we were trying to do in Short's Gardens was in so many ways what I felt I really wanted to do with the rest of my life: and so grew for me that sense of calling which led to ordination and full time ministry in the Church of England.

So you will understand how grateful I am to God and to the Mission, and to Lionel, and to some of the characters he describes in this book. As you read some of Lionel's descriptions of the things he has seen and the ways in which God has used him, Joan and his family, if you find yourself quietly praising God and, like me, gently wiping a tear from your eye, then I feel sure that Lionel will think that all his hard work in writing this book has been worthwhile. Praise God!

INTRODUCTION

In Ecclesiastes 12:12 we read, 'Of making many books there is no end' and a certain wit has responded, 'For the reading of many books there is no time'. I trust, however, that you might find some time to read this one. I can honestly say, hand on heart, that I had no personal intention of writing a book on any subject, and most certainly not one about myself. The personal pronoun aspect of such an assignment has never arrested me, as it tends, all too easily, to promote self-aggrandizement. It has taken ten years of hints, suggestions and even requests by friends and acquaintances from all walks of life to persuade me that it might possibly be a good idea to recall something of my life and, in particular, the ministries in which I have been involved, and to put it into book form.

When I took note of the people who were doing the prompting and their backgrounds, I began to take them more seriously. They included London City Mission colleagues, friends and supporters of the Mission, who heard me speak in public and with whom I held private conversations. There were also those who once lived on London's streets and with whom I still have contact. One Sunday, after I had given an address at the Royal Naval College Chapel, Greenwich, a gentleman, while ensuring I had a cup of coffee, introduced himself as 'Just a soldier'. In the course of our conversation he asked me to talk a little about my life in the L.C.M. Then he said, 'I think you should really turn these experiences into a book'. I told him he was the third person that week to make such a suggestion and I promised to give it some consideration. After we had shaken hands and parted, I asked a friend who the gentleman was. 'Oh,' he replied, 'he is General Sir Ian Gourlay, formerly Commandant General of the Royal Marines.' On looking him up in *Who's Who?*, I learned that his many achievements are well documented. 'I'm just a soldier.' Such humility too.

My family have been my most enthusiastic supporters, by keeping me on track and contributing in practical ways to the production of the book. More than this, Julia has typed it and Marion, where needed, has done what she does best and corrected words, phrases and sentences; and how many times have I heard from Joan, 'How's the book coming on?'

It would be difficult to recall situations and conversations in detail without the help of documentation, and this has been available through years of diary-keeping and annual reports required by the L.C.M. In addition I have rechecked facts with some of the people referred to and for this I am grateful that they have filled in some of the gaps. There is danger in having 'the pen of a ready writer' and I have asked the Lord to hold on to the hand that holds the pen.

Finally, in writing this book I want to glorify God and encourage Christians in their faith and ministry as well as help them to win others for Jesus Christ. Please pray to this end even as you read, and may the Holy Spirit bring you into a closer relationship with God.

1

Early Years

You'll find Dolyhir marked on most maps, even though it has little to recommend it to many people. The name Dolyhir means 'long meadow' and is better known in the locality for its limestone quarries. In all its anonymity Dolyhir nestles close to a delightful winding stream at the foot of the hills and is surrounded by farms and cottages. Locals happily cope with the dust and grime of the quarries, knowing that they provide employment for the young men content to spend their lives in the area like their forefathers. This little hamlet, with its population of less than a hundred, just off the A44 and a mile inside the Welsh border, once boasted a busy railway station with its own resident stationmaster and two passenger trains a day. In my day it was part of Radnorshire – sadly now swallowed up by Powys following the merger of many of the Shires. I was born in a little 200-

At 18 months, my preaching tendencies were apparent!

year-old stone cottage, its two-up and two-down small rooms looking across towards the fields to picturesque Hanter Hill in the distance. It was here that I spent my boyhood up to the age of fifteen.

As well as the quarry and railway station, Dolyhir had a football team that played in the North Hereford League and consisted of quarrymen, farmers and railwaymen. Bitter rivals of another local side, Radnor Valley, league and cup clashes were eagerly anticipated and always physically contested. A special football train ran on Saturdays to Kington, Leominster and New Radnor at 2 p.m. and 4 p.m.

A crowd of a hundred – more than three hundred for an important game – would gather to watch the home side. The team changing room was all of four hundred yards away, and doubled as the billiard hall and venue for whist drives. This single-storey room had been known as the Reading Room, having been built by the local squire for the edification of the quarry workers.

Dolyhir cannot boast a church of any denomination, although at one time there was a very small mission hall, which had been built at the beginning of the twentieth century. This meeting place suited a need following the spread of the Christian revival in Wales in 1904–1905 when blessing came to many parts of the principality, mainly through Evan Roberts, a young man upon whom the powerful Spirit of God came as a result of a consciousness of sin in his life and his desire to serve Him. Much of the principality was affected spiritually and morally as the revival took hold, and although its effects were seen mainly in the south, some isolated parts of mid-Wales were also influenced. The nearest Nonconformist chapel was Yardro, just over a mile away, with the Anglican church of St Stephen's, Old Radnor, the same distance in the opposite direction. Old Radnor means in Welsh, Pen-y-Craig, 'the summit of the rock', the summit in question rising 840 feet above sea level. The old church dates from the fifteenth and early sixteenth centuries but has some features thought to belong to an earlier thirteenth-century place of worship.

The divide between 'church' and 'chapel' was being breached and in the 1940s the evangelical vicar John Goss both visited and enlisted the help of chapel-goers at the parish church. The word 'Anglican' had a nasty taste to it in Wales during the eighteenth century due to its formality in worship and the tendency towards Roman Catholicism, as well as, in some instances, the worldly behaviour of its clergy.

People born in Dolyhir and its environs have no easily recognizable accent: slightly mongrel, it combined the singsong of the Welsh with the harsher sound of the Herefordshire native. Barely fourteen miles away you will hear the softer-enunciating Welsh lilt in Llandrindod Wells or Builth Wells. Dolyhirites also have a vocabulary of their own such as 'wonna' for won't, 'anna' for hasn't, 'canna' for can't and 'a' (as in band) for yes. Like many country places, people 'from off', as they were called, were viewed with suspicion and were only accepted, if ever, after many years. There were exceptions, like a new stationmaster or vicar or headteacher, whose badges of office ensured they were quickly absorbed into the community. There was, however, a good community spirit and where help was needed, it always seemed to be available.

E-mail, fax machines, mobile telephones and other modern communication aids have nothing to compare with Dolyhir's 'bush telegraph' system. Everyone knew everyone and everything; what was not fact was invented, quickly circulated and embroidered. If Mrs — was expecting her fifth in six years, nobody waited for an official announcement; news was out and if the postman didn't spread it, the grocer, the butcher or the baker would. Scandal was not uncommon, particularly when somewhat 'unexpected' babies made their entrance into the community. Likenesses were compared and 'fathers' were traced, even though there were brave attempts at cover-ups. Remember, there was no DNA testing in those days; paternity was decided as follows, 'They say so-and-so is expecting again and that --- is the father', although we never knew the identity of 'they'. Then, in due course, there was careful scrutiny of the newborn's features in order to ascertain paternity. Return visits to the vicinity by anyone who had moved away were always noted, and it was expected that the 'wanderer' would call on a number of people and reminisce about bygone days as well as catch up on current news.

When I was born in 1933, the First World War had been over for fifteen years, and numbers of local 'boys' had been called up. Some, sadly, never returned and their names could be seen on the War Memorial at Old or New Radnor. Others could, and sometimes did, tell their stories of the Somme, Ypres, Passchendaele and Hill 60. My early interest in the Great War was fostered by these men, who recalled the mud, murder and mismanagement which threw away the lives of a whole generation of young men. I have in my possession a large bronze medallion sent by the War Office to my grandparents on the death of their son, Garnett. He was blown up during the last big offensive of the war in August 1918, and news of his death was received on the first Armistice Day. Like many thousands of his comrades the brief details of his death housed in the War Office conclude with the words, 'No known grave'.

Despite never having met my Uncle Garnett (my brother incidentally was named after him), somehow I felt I knew him and was proud of him, particularly when his name was read out each Armistice Sunday as we stood around the Cenotaph overlooking the Radnor Valley. We promised to 'remember them' but I wonder how real those brave young men seem today to the new generation that gathers annually. When I last visited the Celtic Cross Cenotaph on its granite plinth, the names inscribed were fading. What would my paternal grandfather say? A stonemason, he helped build the memorial to his son.

Death was real to me in those days and was brought even closer when, as a little boy of four, I was lifted up to view my grandfather in his coffin. I had happy memories of the times I sat on granddad's knee, pulled his moustache and had him tell me stories. My mother was often called upon to 'lay out' the dead, as most people still died at home in the 1930s and 1940s. It was commonplace to receive a call in the early hours to 'Come and see to mum or dad, or even Sir Douglas (Duff Gordon).' The only benefit was that Mum got a 'tip' for doing it. Then I suddenly lost two school friends, both killed by an unexploded bomb. Roy, one of the two, had promised the day before to come and play with me, on the day he was killed. Two quarrymen were killed at the rock face and, again, this little community was plunged into grief. Somehow these tragedies brought us all closer together, for a while anyway.

I thought deeply about these things, about heaven and the life hereafter, of eternity and God, not to mention the brevity of life. This, I am sure, prepared me for a deeper understanding of biblical truth as well as a sensitivity towards those who are in grief and loss. Before I even reached my teens I was familiar with Bible verses such as: 'O death, where is thy sting? O grave, where is thy victory?' (1 Cor. 15:55 KJV), 'I am the resurrection and the life, says the Lord' (John 11:25) and 'In my Father's house are many mansions' (John 14:2 KJV). These verses were seeds sown in a young mind ready to bear fruit in later years, and it was as if God was preparing me to bring such truths before congregations at funerals in London and other places around the country.

One outstanding incident comes clearly to mind as I recall those boyhood days, an incident that laid the foundation for my conversion to Christ many years later. It was a sunny day and I was playing in the field opposite the little cottage home when I saw a farm labourer hedging in an adjoining field. It was local preacher John Russell, whom I had also seen standing with a small group in nearby Kington on market days singing hymns, preaching and handing out tracts. Although we boys often laughed at the sincere attempts made to attract shoppers, I secretly admired Mr Russell, whose face always shone as he sang and preached. He had to use his lunch hour to do this and would ride the five miles on his motorcycle, with his Bible strapped to the pillion seat.

However, that day I decided I would sing to him. I even remember what I sang: 'The sands of time are sinking, the dawn of heaven breaks'. Don't ask me why I chose this somewhat solemn hymn, but it was enough to cause John to stop and listen. By this time I was standing at his hedge but just a little lower down from him. He made his way to a point opposite, saying with his familiar smile, 'Young man, I'm going to pray for you; I'm going to pray that God will use that voice in his service.' I learned years later that he did just that, and his prayers were answered. It was to be more than twenty years later, when I was invited to preach in the open air at Llandrindod Wells, before I saw John Russell again. There he was standing at the front of the crowd, his Bible under his arm and the largest smile on his face. What a happy reunion that was! Then, years later, while speaking in Hereford, I told the story in order to encourage people to pray for children. After the meeting a lady came up to me saying she too recalled the story, informing me that John Russell was her husband.

My subject that day in Llandrindod Wells was 'lost and found' based on the frightening experience I had as a boy of four in the same town. I had wandered off and got lost, only to be found by a policeman who handed me over to my uncle who at the time was the Chief of Police for mid-Wales. I suppose I could eventually have found my way back to my great grandmother's house by using a number of routes. However, I could only be 'found' spiritually one way, through repentance and faith in Christ as presented in the Gospel.

Among the unique features of Dolyhir and its vicinity was its humour. Situational, it was associated with certain individuals. Old men like Harry Payne who seemed to have worn the same clothes all his life, smoked a clay pipe even though the stem had broken, and who tickled trout. He grew his fingernails until they resembled talons and spat accurately between the bars of the Reading Room fire grate. Old Harry was, on one occasion, the silent listener to the comments of a group of teenage boys who were making detrimental remarks about girls. When asked for his opinion Harry replied, 'Well, I never say anything against women because my mother was a woman.' End of discussion.

My grandfather, Lewis Ball, who would easily be included on any list of local characters, was a frequent visitor to the pub at Old Radnor – The Harp Inn. He had known better days as when he led the singing at Gore Chapel near Walton with the use of a tuning fork, now in my possession. His fondness for drink, however, meant he was often the worse for it, and he could sometimes be found lying on the roadside having fallen from his bicycle. On one occasion he was seen by the local vicar who, as he passed on horseback, enquired, 'Drunk again Ball?', to which granddad replied, 'Be ya Vicar, so be I'. He treated his family cruelly when in drink, and my father often had to physically restrain him when my grandmother, who formerly had been a lady's companion, was at the receiving end of his fits of temper.

Stories of local people and events were handed down from generation to generation and related as groups congregated at weekends in selected meeting places such as Dolyhir Bridge, Walton, Old Radnor and Gladestry. Some of these stories undoubtedly bore more than hints of exaggeration. I fear, however, that the tellers of such legends have long since disappeared.

Like most people, I suppose, I remember my first day at school. In my case it was at Old Radnor School at the top of the hill between Dolyhir and Walton and across the road from the old Church of St Stephen. My father had also attended the same school and remembered clearly the strict and efficient head, the redoubtable Mr Stone. During the first week in January 1939 the weather was cold and the roads icy as Gwyneth Morgan, from the farm up the road and due to leave school soon, held my hand as well as that of her brother Austin, who was also making his debut at the school. I'm not sure why my brother didn't take me; perhaps he was so keen to get to school that he ran the two miles past the quarries and up the hill, or maybe he chose to meet his pals and take the shorter route along the fields.

My introduction to school life coincided with the arrival of the new headmaster, Mr Roberts, a man who was not just a teacher but an educator in many subjects, and equally as keen on good discipline as any of his predecessors. Although we children often reeled at his stentorian tones, he had a great deal of influence on us and, in later life, I realized just how much I had learned from him. I never found school boring because 'the boss', as we called him, and his staff of two always made lessons interesting. Arithmetic, as it was known in those days, was high on his list of priorities as a daily lesson, as were English, music and what we called Scripture. We learned by heart whole passages from the Bible, and I remember committing to memory the first five chapters of Acts. It was as though I was being prepared even in those days for the ministry twenty years later.

I remember sitting the eleven-plus examination for entrance to Presteigne Grammar School, during which the invigilator, the local publican and Old Radnor Home Guard's equivalent of Captain Mainwaring, wasn't above giving an answer or two to struggling students. Apart from my first two terms at Presteigne, I found life hard going academically except in music, history and English, mainly because I didn't apply myself to those other subjects with which I had problems. I enjoyed drama and played parts in school plays including Lorenzo in *The Merchant of Venice* and Snout in *A Midsummer Night's Dream*. I played first-eleven football and cricket, and represented the school at athletics as a sprinter. Hindsight informs me that, had I put as much effort into studying as I did into sport, I might have passed a few more exams and even become university material.

There was always plenty to do out of school hours too; it was safe to roam the countryside, climb the hills and, of course, play football and cricket. During the years 1939 to 1945 we hardly realized there was a war on, although there were army camps at nearby Harpton and Downton, both of which were vacated overnight in readiness for the D-Day landings in France in 1944. The nearest we came to any real danger was when two German landmines were unloaded over New Radnor, making deep craters in Smatcher Hill. Had they landed in the village, the place would have been blown apart, resulting in the loss of many lives. The local Home Guard (Dad's Army) did its bit, and Dad rose to the exalted rank of second lieutenant; he took it all very seriously as did his colleagues. It was the least he could do, having been turned down when he volunteered for the Forces.

Before owning a bicycle I walked (or ran) everywhere, even as far as Kington five miles away, especially to go to the Picture House. When I became the proud possessor of a 'bike', it was an A.S.P. – all spare parts – and I would ride for miles to all sorts of events, sometimes with a cigarette packet sticking through the spokes in order to make it sound like a car.

I've already referred to the incident in the field and the promise of John Russell to pray for me. Well, there was another significant moment in my life as a boy, which stands out in my memory. At the end of the war schoolmaster Roberts had organized a coach trip to London with a special visit to the Houses of Parliament and I had hoped I might go. It was not to be. My mother told me that they just couldn't afford the fare but she added, as if by way of promise, if not prophecy, 'Never mind, you'll go to London one day.' Hence the title of this book.

The days of my childhood are clear in my mind. The summers were always hot and long and the winters cold. Snow lay on the ground for two months in 1947 and our old cat brought in a rabbit ten days running (not the same rabbit) when we were cut off and short of food. I used to pull our daughters' legs with the apocryphal story that, in the winter of 1940, which was equally severe, we would sit round a candle and when the weather was unbearable Dad would light it. In contrast, the summer of 1947 was glorious and the late great cricketer Denis Compton scored 3,816 runs and eighteen centuries in the sun for Middlesex and England.

Breaking away from this very rural, tightly knit, environment was not easy. The Second War took away some of the young men, and a number didn't return. Some met their future wives during their Forces days and set up home in other parts of the country. National Service ensured that this trend continued after the end of the war, a trend which meant that the community lost many of its young people. I often think of them. Where are they? Have they heard the true Gospel? If so, have they responded?

I think it was a great surprise to many when I decided, at fifteen, to join the RAF as a Boy Entrant. The hardest part of such a move was not getting into the RAF but getting out of such a close-meshed community and leaving a secure loving home for a communal life with little freedom. But life in the RAF appealed to me and I felt I could wear the uniform with pride, so I sent off my application forms and waited. Within a week postman Tippings brought the reply from the Air Ministry and I was called for interviews and tests.

Being a Boy Entrant, however, was a bit like going to a boarding school; there were lessons every day, all related to the chosen trade, and plenty of opportunity for sport and recreation. Eight weeks holiday a year plus two long weekends and a fortnight's summer camp, all added up to a well-organized programme. The weekly pay scale for recruits was five shillings (25p) with a two-and-sixpence (12½p) increase after twelve months. After eighteen months' training each Boy Entrant, hopefully, had a worthwhile trade that could lead to a long career.

I had never been further from home than Swansea, so the prospect of four days' 'attestation' on the famous Battle of Britain airfield at Hornchurch in Essex was somewhat daunting. I had to be there by midday, so this meant travelling overnight. At least I could get the train from Dolyhir to Hereford and change to a night train that was due in at Paddington in the early hours of the morning. As the train drew near London I realized how big the capital was. Why couldn't I see Wembley Stadium, the Albert Hall, Big Ben and Highbury, the Arsenal football ground, as the train pulled into the smoke?

Paddington Station was so big, so noisy. I stood on the platform feeling alone and lost. What was the prophecy Mum had made when she told me she couldn't afford to pay my coach fare on the school trip to London? She said, 'Never mind, you'll go to London one day.' I think that was a promise too. 'Remember,' Mum had said, 'you've got a tongue in your head, use it.' So I did. 'When's the next train to Elm Park?' I asked, clutching my travel instructions given me by Percy Griffiths the stationmaster at Dolyhir. 'They run all the time, mate,' said the porter. I was soon walking through the main gates at RAF Hornchurch and into a different world. What were the two pieces of advice given by Mum and Dad? From Dad, 'Watch your money and watch your friends.' 'Oh yes,' Mum added, 'and say your prayers.' Well, 'watch and pray' I suppose. Wise counsel for a fifteen-year-old then, and just as relevant today.

The next three days were spent taking tests in educational subjects and being assessed for the most suitable trade. Listening to Morse code and frequency notes was obviously related to wireless telegraphy, as was handwriting legibility and neatness. I was pretty confident I had done well and returned home to wait for my letter of acceptance, anticipating RAF life would begin at the end of September 1949.

2

LIFE IN THE RAF

Within days I received the following communication from the Air Ministry:

> 'You have been accepted for training as a Boy Entrant to become a U/T Telegraphist. You are asked to report to RAF Locking near Weston-super-Mare on Tuesday, 27 September 1949 for initial training, then be posted to No. 3 Radio School, Compton Bassett.'

That was to be the last occasion for ten years when I would be asked by the RAF to do anything; from then on I was **told**. I might as well go, I thought, since I'm due for National Service in October 1951 anyway. So, with my little leather suitcase in my hand, I bade farewell to Mum, Dad, the ever-helpful stationmaster, Percy Griffiths, and the vicar, the Rev. John Goss. The little train pulled out of Dolyhir Station and I was bound for a lifetime of adventure in the big world. As usual Dad went home to lunch and neither he nor Mum spoke; they just sat there wondering what the future held for their youngest son. Dad mounted his cycle and rode back to work, and Mum ... well, she sat down and wrote me a letter – that was typical!

So I became a number and a name, 1922639 Boy Entrant Ball, L. R. 8th Entry, spent my sixteenth birthday at Locking, then in two weeks moved on to RAF Compton Bassett near Calne in Wiltshire. I had never experienced communal living before; twenty-five in a Nissen hut with a few square inches to call my own. An iron bedstead with three thin square 'biscuits', five rough blankets and two sheets, all of which had to be neatly folded daily. Every item of service-issue kit had to be on view uniformly on the bed or showing through the open door of a wooden locker. Webbing equipment must be blancoed, brass buttons shining brightly and boots gleaming like patent leather, having been 'bulled' up through hours of spit and polish. Water from the tap wouldn't do: it must be good honest spit rubbed into the leather using a circular motion.

Reveille was sounded at 0630 hours, not with the dulcet tones of a trumpet or the gradual crescendo of an orchestral record played through a loudspeaker, but by the raucous, ranting Corporal who, on entering the hut in marching fashion, kicked over the fire buckets and tipped over the nearest bed complete with occupant. Even in the middle of winter, according to these foul mouthed, seemingly less than human creatures, the sun was always 'burning your eyeballs out'.

Washing facilities in those days were inevitably in another building, so this meant come hail or sunshine you braved the elements and queued up for a basin which had already been used by the swifter mortals and who, more often than not, knew nothing of cleaning them after use.

Breakfast was from 0730–0800 hours and you queued up outside the cookhouse; if you weren't quick, this was especially unpleasant in the winter. You booked a seat (or part of a bench) stood at the servery, were given a dollop of cold porridge, a floating fried egg, cold and crisp fried bread and two pieces of curled-up fried bacon which, if you didn't hold your breath, would slide off the plate. You balanced an enamel mug of tea on one plate and all this was a waste of time because, when you arrived back at your table, some thief had made off with your 'irons' (knife, fork and spoon). There was nothing else for it but to resort to nature's provision for eating – fingers. Then you had to try washing your cutlery (if you still owned them) in cold, greasy, communal water. Worse was to come: you had no eating irons to lay out for the kit inspection. You could be sure they would be missed, and consequently you would be in trouble.

We were on parade at 0815 unless we were required for billet orderly, in which case we made sure the hut was 'standing to attention' ready for inspection at 0900 hours. We were in class by 0845 where we tackled such subjects as maths, English, elementary radio, Morse and typewriting. 'Square bashing' was part of our daily programme, as was physical training. 'Discipline begins on the barrack square', we were told, and we believed it. Those .303 rifles were very heavy and in the winter you were not allowed to wear your woollen gloves or the thing would slide from your grasp; dropping your rifle while on parade was a chargeable offence, as you were rendering yourself defenceless. Failure to cope with the rigours of rifle drill often led to running round the square with the rifle above your head – it was sheer torture. Speaking of torture reminds me of the hairdresser they called 'Sweeney Todd'. He really was the next thing to the demon barber of Fleet Street. It would all start with a parade dialogue that went like this: Warrant Officer – 'Am I hurting you boy?' 'No, sir.' 'Then I should be, I'm standing on your hair; get it cut, now.' Next day, the same question would be met with the answer: 'I had one yesterday, sir' and the response, 'Well, get another one today' – and at six old pence (2½p) a time!

I decided to heed the advice given to me, 'work hard, play hard, and trench hard' (Trenchard being a founding father of the RAF). I played for the boys' football team and later the station team.

From a camp of 3000, and at sixteen, to be one of only two non-professionals in the squad was quite an achievement. (Those were the days of National Service when young men between eighteen and twenty were automatically called up.) Playing alongside players who on Saturdays would be turning out for Aston Villa, Manchester City, Stoke City, Scunthorpe and Raith Rovers was an unexpected honour.

We learned to live with one another, help those who were slowest (and scruffiest) for their good and the honour of the 'glorious 8th' and make our own entertainment in order to cope with the boredom of off-duty time. Camaraderie was of the highest order and squabbles few and far between. My particular pal was Roy Chandler and we were to be together for the next four years.

Soon I was given one stripe, and then two and a room of my own, and no more rifle drill. Then my third stripe came and I was in charge of three hundred boys. I loved it, barking out orders on the parade ground, leading the wing through the streets of Calne for Battle of Britain and Remembrance Day parades, and training new recruits in rifle and foot drill. Then, at the end of it all, I became Parade Commander of the combined Yatesbury and Compton Bassett passing out parade before a large audience of dignitaries, including Mum and Dad.

It is my guess that being the Sergeant Boy Parade Commander for the passing out parade was the dream of every Boy Entrant. At seventeen years of age controlling a parade of five hundred young men, including the 8th Entry from nearby RAF Yatesbury, with the station military band, and presenting a forty-minute ceremonial, gave me a real sense of power and pride. I can still remember every word of command, visualize every movement and hear every piece of music played by the band. At the end of the ceremonial, I marched forward to the saluting-base, saluted and requested permission to march the parade off the parade ground. The reviewing officer, Air Vice Marshall J. D. Hardman, stepped down from the dais, shook me by the hand as he congratulated me, and granted the necessary permission. I gave my final orders as the Senior Entry Sergeant Boy and marched off to the tune of 'Auld Lang Syne', and into the future, a qualified tradesman.

Leaving was a little like leaving school all over again, although this time I had no choice in the matter of my immediate future. I was to report to RAF Rudloe Manor just a few miles away, where I would be working underground on a fully operational signals unit.

Being congratulated by
Air Vice Marshal Hardman
at the passing out Parade †

During my two years at Rudloe just off the A4, I became quite involved in station camp activities, the drama group, and the football and athletics teams. It was while based here that I had a trial with Swindon Town, who were anxious to sign the quick seventeen-year-old winger on amateur forms. I turned down their request mainly because I didn't have the confidence in my own ability, so I satisfied myself with playing in the camp team on Wednesdays and a local village team on Saturdays.

I made some good friends during my Rudloe days and I am still in touch with some of them: Bill Thompson, Bernard Fowlds and Mick Harris. Mick used to talk to me about his conversion to Christ, the Bible and the little mission hall he attended back home in Thornton Heath, Surrey; his life matched the things about which he spoke, and I began to respect and admire him. He shared a room with Bernard and often when I went in he would be reading his Bible, which was obviously his daily habit.

It was through Mick that I came to hear about the London City Mission. Eventually he took me to his home and together we went to a local mission hall that was under the superintendency of James Atwell, a London City Missionary. The little building was teeming with young people to whom Jesus Christ was very real; one of them was Joan Spencer who, five years later, would become my wife. The enthusiasm of these young folk impressed itself on my heart and I could hardly believe they gave all their spare moments to attending the little hall; to me they appeared as one happy family. They worshipped together, played together, went to summer camps together, cycled together and even went out on the street with their brass band, gave out leaflets and made their presence felt in the district. Although I was prepared to label them fanatics, I held a secret admiration for them and wished I could be like them.

As I left the hall on that first visit, I was confronted by the little wife of the City Missionary who challenged me with the words, 'Are you a believer?' 'Oh yes.' I replied, which was an honest answer; although on reflection it only expressed head knowledge rather than a testimony to a personal heart relationship with Jesus Christ. This brief encounter with Mrs Atwell took just ten seconds but it was sufficient to remain imprinted on my mind for at least another four years until I did something about it, but more of that later.

In April 1953, the year of Everest, the Coronation and the Stanley Matthews cup final, I was posted to Germany as part of the British Forces of Occupation. I caught the troop train at Liverpool Street Station and on arrival at Harwich, boarded the Empire Wansbeck, a large ship specially assigned to Forces personnel, on which, I have to admit, I was seasick for the first and only time. Then came the overland train journey from the Hook of Holland to RAF Buckeburg where I was to serve for the next twenty months.

Again I became very involved with station activities such as football and athletics but never neglected my 'church' life. I became the organist for RAF services held in the local German church, but all the while I was aware that Christianity was not as personally real to me as it should have been. I resisted any call to repent of sin and trust Christ as my personal Saviour, treating it as an affront to my pride and 'churchianity'. God's Holy Spirit was not going to give up on me, however, and every now and then the challenge to follow Christ would come from one direction or another. It was to be another two years before I was finally cornered. Sometimes people are 'arrested' by God in the most dramatic ways as in the case of the Apostle Paul in Acts chapter 9. At other times the process is painful through an accident or other tragedy. In my case God was gentle and patient with a very slow learner, giving me the opportunity to think things through. It is recorded of our Lord Jesus that he knew what was in man, and this is still true. My point of surrender and the circumstances surrounding it are described in another chapter.

Life in general during my tour of duty in Germany was enjoyable. There was plenty of football, cricket and athletics, and these often involved flying from one venue to another. Consequently the next two years went by fairly quickly. In 1954, however, during a visit to Thornton Heath, I was to be introduced to my future wife, Joan Spencer. We agreed to correspond but this lasted only a short while as she, true to her Christian conscience, felt she should not continue an attachment to someone who was not a committed Christian.

In January 1955 I was posted to Sundern following promotion, and caught up with some old pals like Bill Price and Graham Adams (he later became a qualified FIFA coach and managed the Korean national team). In July 1955 I returned to the UK, having been posted to RAF Northolt in charge of the signals traffic office, during which time Joan and I met once more and subsequently saw quite a lot of each other. I was then made captain of the station football team and was offered a trial with Crystal Palace but declined, having signed for Harrow Town (now Harrow Borough) in the Spartan League. Then came a surprise posting to RAF Wattisham in Suffolk. This amounted to another RAF 'joke'. Having been given a London posting, I was now on my way again after only two months.

3

CONVERTED AT LAST

RAF Wattisham was a large Fighter Command station that had three squadrons based there, and I was to be NCO in charge of the Signals Traffic Section. As usual I threw myself into the station's activities, becoming choirmaster and organist at the Anglican church and, after a trial game, went straight into the station football team. A well-trained unit, the team consisted of the best players from a station of 3000 personnel; we won the league and the cup and would have coped well with most third or second division teams of the Football League. The manager of Ipswich Town, Alf Ramsey, later to lead England to victory in the 1966 World Cup, wanted to sign seven members of the team including myself; but weekends were too precious to give up so I was among those who declined.

Friday evenings saw a fleet of coaches leaving the camp for London and every other week I would be among them. Joan and I had met once more but by this time I had begun to give more serious thought to Christian commitment. We began to attend Thornton Heath Memorial Hall, Pawson's Road, which was parented by West Croydon Baptist Church. The hall was under the superintendence of a young banker, Ted Gould. Ted was a methodical, wise and efficient leader, who would not claim to be a preacher but led very much by example. He and his wife Ena were to become two of our closest friends.

Sunday, 1 January 1956 was not only the beginning of a new year but, for me, the start of a new life, that is new life in Jesus Christ. Normally I would be reluctant to leave Joan in order to catch the eleven o'clock coach from King's Cross to Wattisham. That night was different. I had business with God, serious business. I hurried on to the coach, settled down in a window seat and, as I ate the sandwiches Joan had prepared, I willed the three-hour journey to be quicker than usual. Usually I read the Sunday paper, then dropped off into a doze, but it was not possible that night. I was under conviction of sin, not any particular sin, just SIN – original sin. It wasn't the sermon I heard at the mission or any verse of Scripture that made me feel uneasy. It was a deep sense of guilt and an urge to confess to God that I was in need of forgiveness. I knew why Jesus died on the cross – it was for sin, the sin of the world and more personally, my sin. I knew I only had to confess my sin, believe the Gospel, seek forgiveness and ask Christ to become my own personal Saviour, and God would be true to His word that He would forgive. I also knew that my attitude, life and allegiance would have to change too, as expressed in 2 Corinthians 5:17: 'If any man is in Christ he is a new creation.'

The coach arrived back at camp at the usual time, 0200hrs. I went into my little room, dropped to my knees and knew I was in the presence of the great God of salvation. I poured out my soul to God in repentance and claimed the promise that He would be faithful and forgive my sin and cleanse me from all unrighteousness. In addition, I promised I would tell the first person I met what had happened. Come the daylight and I remembered my promise, but I also remembered the commanding officer was likely to be the first person I would meet, as he often walked that way from his residence to the headquarters building. Well, that morning it wasn't to be the redoubtable group captain H. I. Edwards V.C. but another airman whom I stopped and to whom I said, 'I want to tell you that I was saved last night – I became a Christian.' 'Praise God!' said the other fellow, 'I'm a Christian too.'

I immediately joined the Thursday evening Bible class conducted by a faithful member of an Ipswich Brethren assembly, Tom Stiling. Tom was working methodically, verse by verse Brethren-style, through Paul's second letter to Timothy, and soon I was able to contribute and began to enjoy the discussions.

The camp first-eleven football team won the cup and I scored one of the goals and provided another, once again attracting the attention of Ipswich Town scouts, the game being played on the Town ground at Portman Road. I was described as being among the fastest wingers ever to play there. In the summer I won the station 100 and 200-yard sprints and soon found myself competing against some of the country's top runners in RAF championships. Alas, I was too small for sprinting at the highest level and lacked the power required to beat the best. Looking back, I always felt I had chosen the wrong distances and should have concentrated on the half mile and mile races; my father, incidentally, equalled the British quarter mile record in the late 1920s, so he could run a bit too.

'Lionel could do much better' was a regular comment in my school reports and I regretted not having tried harder. However, I decided to make up for it by studying for some 'O' levels, which I passed. More importantly, I grew spiritually and owed a great deal to Tom Stiling. I joined the SASRA (Soldiers' and Airmen's Scripture Readers Association) and got to know the secretary, Captain Sidney May, who also encouraged me to memorize the Scriptures.

Music continued to play an important part in my life and I joined the Croydon Male Voice Gospel Choir. What a thrill it was to sing the Gospel and to be doing it in the way which appealed to all Welshmen – singing in a male voice choir. Alfred Vickery, who did his apprenticeship in the Salvation Army, was the conductor, and he encouraged me to play and conduct. 'Marvellous and Wonderful', 'We'll All Be There', 'Since Jesus Came into My Heart', 'Burdens are Lifted' and 'Jesus Satisfies Me' were among the favourites of the day, and in those days there was no lack of engagements as people loved to hear men singing the Gospel. Every choir member had to be prepared to give a testimony and usually one of us conducted the epilogue too. Once a year choirs from all over the south east of England sang to a filled Royal Albert Hall. What a marvellous experience! The grand organ fascinated me, and I marvelled at the organist's ability to cope with something that looked like the flight deck of a great airliner. Would I one day have the chance to play this famous instrument? This was just a dream then, but one that would come true later.

The year 1957 was to be a very special one for Joan and me, for we had become engaged in August 1956 and fixed the wedding for September 28 1957. All through that year Joan and I prepared for our big day. She worked out our finances – as she has done through our married life – and the day was just as happy as we had anticipated. Geoffrey King, the minister of West Croydon Baptist Church, conducted the wedding and there was a small reception at Joan's home, 7 Fountain Road, Thornton Heath. Joan's mum and a neighbour had saved up much of the food for the meal and the small front room could barely hold the few relatives and friends who came.

Myself & Joan on our wedding day
28th September 1957 †

Joan's dad put on a brave face for his only daughter, with the emphasis on the 'face'. He had to have all his teeth out and his replacements weren't ready. He did very well, trying to fill out his cheeks for the camera even though he had threatened to spoil it all.

I thanked God for Joan that day and have done so ever since. I do not exaggerate when I say that, without her strength, practical and spiritual support, and self-sacrifice, I could not have fulfilled my ministry nearly so effectively, particularly in those early L.C.M. days when life was far from easy.

A week's honeymoon was all we could manage and we spent five days in Hastings at a Christian hotel for slightly less than £8 in today's money, to include B & B and evening meal. Joan was back in the office on the Monday and I reported to Wattisham by 0800 hours on the same day.

September 1957 was special for another reason. Both Joan and I were baptized by immersion three weeks before the wedding. So much was to happen for us in 'September'. I joined the RAF in September 1949, and was baptized and married in September 1957. In September 1959 I was to leave the RAF, and in September 1960 I joined the London City Mission. In September 1961 our daughter Marion was born, then in September 1990, on the anniversary of our wedding, our first grandchild, William, was born.

The RAF, predictable for its unpredictability, had a shock awaiting my return to duty. I discovered I had been placed on the PWR (preliminary warning roster). The dreaded list of overseas postings, surely not! With under two years to go to demob? Oh, yes! And destination – Christmas Island!

I considered this pretty unfair and even unscriptural (Deut. 24:5: 'If a man has recently married, he must not be sent to war or have any other duty laid on him. For one year he is to be free to stay at home and bring happiness to the wife he has married') but I hadn't the nerve to protest. The whole painful process of preparation took four months. There was some consolation when

I was posted to Uxbridge during October and this meant frequent visits to see Joan. We were quickly learning that becoming unitedly committed to serving the Lord didn't always lead to everything falling into place just as we wished.

I was given three weeks embarkation leave but was recalled after two weeks, and Joan and I made our tearful farewells. Four months married and then separated for three and possibly more could be a recipe for disaster. This, however, has always been one of the hazards of life in the Forces and had to be faced. Both Joan and I believed in the word of Scripture that God would watch between us while we were away from each other (Gen. 31:49).

So I was once again on number-one platform at Paddington Station where I had been many times before – mostly on happier occasions waiting for the train bound for the West Country. Never mind, I thought; there are others in the same boat, so to speak. They were on the same train anyway, all going to Christmas Island like me. The RAF, however, had a nasty way of rubbing in the salt: most of them were travelling to the same camp but in order to 'clear' for 'demob'. How could the RAF be so heartless? You wait and see!

'Who was Jacob's wife?' asked a 'demob-happy' travelling companion. I felt like giving him an answer like Elizabeth Taylor or Diana Dors. I told him the answer and turned it into an opportunity to talk about the Bible but, truthfully, I was more concerned about the young wife I was leaving back in London.

I joined scores of others at the dispersal point near Gloucester. Transit camps are a sort of 'no man's land' where very little happens except the constant round of visits to medical centres; there you slowly shuffle, hands on hips, past a doctor with a needle, as he tries to convince you that it won't hurt and an injection is necessary if you are to stay alive for the next few months.

Since my training included air-to-ground wireless communications using the old transmitter and receiver equipment, I had completed many hours of flying duties. In those days Ansons and Hastings were still in use, and I had even experienced being thrown around in an Auster piloted by an army captain who feared nothing it seemed. Flying in severe wintry conditions was different (Britain was covered in snow) and those of us bound for Christmas Island were, to say the least, apprehensive. On the minds of everyone was the fact that just three weeks earlier the aircraft carrying the famous Busby Babes of Manchester United had crashed on take-off at Munich, killing thirty-three people including eleven players.

February weather conditions prevented our scheduled take-off from Southend so we were taken to Heathrow. As the Air Charter London Skymaster taxied along the runway then lifted away from the London lights, we were aware that all was not well. The pilot informed us we were returning to Heathrow. There was ice on the wings and no chances were being taken. The ice being cleared, another attempt was made but this was too risky so, once more, we returned to base. Some of us prayed as we reached for the sky a third time and headed west for Shannon, Canada, San Francisco, Honolulu and Christmas Island.

Three days later our aircraft circled round a sandy, tented compound, which we were told was Christmas Island. We landed bumpily but safely on the makeshift runway and made our way, with our tongues hanging out, to the refreshment tent. We longed for an ice-cold drink but all we got was warm pineapple juice. Imagine what it felt like, full marching order with the temperature more than 100°F in the shade (what shade?) and only warm pineapple juice to drink! I flopped down on my safari bed and asked myself why on earth I ever put my signature to that piece of paper in September 1949.

Whenever I felt homesick and far from home I have always looked for a church. I wandered through the rows of tents until I found the one with a cross above its door. Inside I knelt to pray;

after all, God would know how I was feeling. As I opened my eyes I saw an airman standing nearby. 'Hello,' he said holding out his hand, 'I'm John and I'm a Christian'. This was music to my ears. I was to learn he had been converted to Christ through a London City Missionary in North London. As we talked I noticed an old piano, so I walked over to it and began to play. Some notes refused to respond and most of those that did were out of tune, but I was happy enough just to be making music. Just then the camp padre, who lost no time in telling me off for playing the piano without permission, interrupted me. It was ironic that I was playing 'What a friend we have in Jesus'. As he walked away I saw, sticking from his hip pocket, a bottle of whisky, and quickly decided that maybe he was touched by the wrong kind of spirit.

Within days I was given good news and bad news as I was to be posted to Honolulu on the Hawaiian Island of Oahu. At the time I would have liked to have seen at least one hydrogen bomb test but forty years later I am feeling rather pleased not to have been anywhere nearer than Honolulu, judging by the reports of some of my colleagues who are suffering from the effect of radiation produced through those controversial tests. But what about the bad news? This plum posting to Honolulu was for eleven months, not three. Waikiki beach, Pearl Harbor and all such an assignment had to offer was no compensation for separation from Joan, but I had to make the best of it. We were always being told, 'If you can't take a joke, you shouldn't have joined.' This was one joke I didn't consider funny.

All things considered, serving with the United States Air Force turned out to be an enjoyable experience and, in particular, being involved with the local Base church. For me the outstanding memory was the opportunity to study the Bible and have the encouragement of a young American, Ron Peters. Ron introduced me to an organization called Navigators whose main emphasis lay in memorizing the Scriptures. I spent hours reading my Bible and learning and applying Bible verses. I assure you there was much more to life for me than lying in the sun and working up a tan (would you believe it, I never went into the water above my waist? – I can't swim). This was good preparation for my future work and proved to be invaluable when I joined the London City Mission where workers in those days specialized in using the Bible in the ministry of personal evangelism. While I was there, I committed to memory more than a hundred texts, knew their contexts and could explain and apply them. I was also involved in the work at the chapel, and the American chaplain and I enjoyed working together.

I have to say that life at Hickham USAF Base wasn't difficult and I was responsible for one of the watches (or shifts). Two H-bombs were tested during my tour of duty and shortly after the second one we were on our way home. After a month's disembarkation leave I was posted to RAF Manston in Kent. With six months to go, I was on my last lap.

My first task at Manston was to reopen the signals centre, make it operational and organize the staff. In addition I started a station library and played in the football team, whose coach was the former Welsh international half-back, Bert Turner. Bert had the dubious distinction of scoring through his own goal while playing for Charlton Athletic against Derby County in the 1946 FA Cup Final. However, he compensated by equalizing within a minute from a free kick. We never reminded him of this doubtful privilege, although some years later he described the experience on a BBC radio sports programme. As well as being the football team coach, Bert was landlord of the Jolly Farmer Inn nearby. He was a pleasant fellow and we often discussed Christian subjects. He had been impressed by the witness of another Charlton colleague, Bert Johnson, an English international, who also played wing half. I was to meet Bert some years later when on deputation for the L.C.M. in Leicester.

Joan's and my thoughts were constantly centred on demobilization from the RAF and, with just six months to go, time would soon pass. I would need a job first before considering some full-time Christian work. Although I enjoyed good fellowship at Cavendish Baptist Church in Ramsgate, and Queens Road Baptist Church in Broadstairs, a weekend pass each Friday saw me return to Waddon near Croydon where Joan and I had rented a small flat.

September eventually arrived and I obtained my final signatures for clearance at Manston, and I was a civilian again after ten years. How strange are God's ways, as forty years later Joan and I would return to Herne Bay near Manston to live in retirement.

My record of service showed me as having good leadership and personal qualities, and my commanding officer described me as being keen, conscientious and very loyal, very religious and extremely suitable for following a career as a religious worker. I also got a Special Commendation for 'Meritorious Service in the Pacific'. Well, that was kind of the RAF! I enjoyed my time in the RAF and without it my Christian service and in particular my days with the City Police would have been the poorer. So it was 'future here I come', a holiday in Cornwall and then look for a job.

There were plenty of positions going in Civvy Street. Teleprinter operators were needed with Esso and I was actually offered shift work at Croydon Airport with a good rate of pay, but that was too close to the RAF so I opted to become a sales clerk in a firm which manufactured bathroom fittings. Football wasn't far from my mind and I signed to play for Croydon Amateurs, and played regularly, but my heart was no longer in the game. Although Joan often watched the Saturday games, it was unfair to expect her to give up her only day off from work to stand on the terraces or touch-line of a football pitch. Then there were two evenings out for training which clashed with the midweek meeting at the mission hall.

Often during a game I would be thinking about spiritual matters, verses from the Bible and talks I had to prepare.

After four months with Croydon, I wrote to the chairman of the club to tell him that the game in which I had scored four goals had to be the last but one. I gave my reasons and two club officials were quickly on the doorstep trying to persuade me to reconsider, but my mind was made up! By this time a young Christian couple, Wilce and Eileen Webb, had taken Joan and me into their home to live in two rooms. We were so grateful to them as this meant limiting their own space, and, with their own little son now four, this was a great sacrifice.

4

The London City Mission

Although I gained good work experience at Metlex Industries in Sumner Road, Croydon, I had made it clear to the managing director that this was very much short term. I became the local secretary for the L.C.M. in Croydon and in a short time while involved, increased the number of people in supporting the Mission's work. Each year a special meeting was held on behalf of the L.C.M. in the Croydon area, and on one of these occasions the missionary speaker was Joseph Currie, who ministered among London's homeless. In story after story he told how he sat with them, gave them food and clothing and cared for them, showing the love of Christ and of His power to save.

Maybe I wasn't prepared to minister to the homeless of London but I felt I could gladly spend my days among London's people in some Christian capacity. I had tried the doors of some other Christian organizations: The Scripture Gift Mission, Scripture Union, The Shaftesbury Society; another, The Glyn Vivian Miners Mission, was looking for a secretary. My thoughts turned once again to the London City Mission. These men (men only in those days) went where people were. I had read F. H. Wrintmore's books on the Mission's work in London and had got to know many missionaries by sight through seeing their photographs. I had met them at Tower Hill and visited their mission halls. Besides there were my good friends – Mick Harris, Stephen Hayles and dear old Jim Atwell, all City Missionaries – who encouraged me to witness for Christ.

I considered attending a weekend conference for prospective City Missionaries but had to cry off as Joan was having her tonsils removed. Then a letter arrived from the London City Mission inviting me for an interview, should I be considering joining. Joan and I gave the possibility a lot of thought and prayer, and felt that I should apply to the L.C.M., so I completed the necessary forms. I was called for an interview with the candidates secretary the Rev. Bob Otway and the L.C.M. committee, and sent for examination by four eminent ministers, Canon Frank Colquhoun, the Rev. Llewelyn Roberts, the Rev. Pryce Lewis and the Rev. Angus McMillan.

Canon Colquhoun tested me on my knowledge of the Bible, asking me to give an overview of the first five chapters of the Epistle to the Romans. I struggled a bit both with the man and his questions and, according to his report, he with me. I still felt that I had given him an adequate run down on Romans 1–5 in spite of what he said. Dear old Llewelyn Roberts, a former theological college principal, wanted to hear my Christian testimony; speaking through a heavy cold, he was anxious to know what led to my conversion. William Pryce Lewis, minister at Trinity Road Chapel, Tooting, was concerned that I knew I was a Christian; could I give proof? I went straight to the Bible. 'Whosoever believes in me has everlasting life' (John 3:16). 'And this is the record that God has given to us eternal life and this life is in his Son. He who has the Son has life...' (1 John 5:11-12). 'If you will believe in your heart that God has raised Him (Jesus) from the dead you will be saved' (Rom. 10:9). Finally, a dour old Scot, the Rev. Angus McMillan, a pioneer of 'dress down', as he slurped a mug of tea, asked, 'What books have you read young man?' I replied, '*Truth for our Time* (Geoffrey King), *Mere Christianity* (C. S. Lewis), and *Elijah* (A. W. Pink)', not that I understood that one very much. I didn't think the reverend gentleman was too impressed, but as we parted company he literally gave me the thumbs up and growled, 'You'll be alright'; and alright I was, for I got through the committee stages – a committee which included the famous General Sir William Dobbie of Malta. Sir William, greatly admired by the late King George VI, was considered to be Malta's inspiration as Governor in protecting the island when faced by Germany's invading forces during the Second World War, a feat that gained Malta the George Cross.

Geoffrey King and the membership at West Croydon Baptist Church commissioned Joan and me on the first Sunday in September 1960 and 'sent us out' to work with the London City Mission. On the Tuesday I was introduced to my trainer, Fred Hughes, and was told I was to do my four months' probation in the Parish of All Saints, Wandsworth. Oh no! I thought, not Church of England! I'd left the Anglican fold; surely they didn't preach the Gospel in the C of E. I soon discovered otherwise.

Fred and Vera Hughes looked after me during the week and I spent five hours a day knocking on doors in the Parish of Holy Trinity – part of the All Saints set-up. Fred was a fine missionary and was well-known in the district as a caring, sincere Christian gentleman. That first door, however, was frightening. 'Lord, don't let there be anyone in', I prayed. There wasn't. 'Thank you, Lord.' Other knocks were answered, and I was glad there were no militant atheists among them; I wouldn't have known what to do, but hoped Fred would. I didn't realise that Fred had the same hopes of me!

Next day I was told to make my own way and work out my own patch. Morning after morning I travelled from Thornton Heath to Clapham Junction and then by bus to Wandsworth. I would then walk up the hill to my district. Each morning at around 10 o'clock I would see an elderly man resting on a seat. I decided I would stop and talk to him. I did this every day for a week until I noticed how badly worn his shoes were. I remembered the account given by Joseph Currie at the L.C.M. meeting. He had seen a man with no socks, so he gave him his own. I didn't feel I could give the old chap my shoes there and then, but I had a pair at home and the next day gave them to him; this was the breakthrough. I soon gained access to his home, met his wife and paid regular visits. The old man became ill and could no longer leave the house. I soon was able to read the Bible to him and he trusted Christ as his Saviour.

Psalm 51 was written by King David when under conviction following his adulterous liaison with Bathsheba, and the murder (by sending him into the front line of battle) of Uriah, Bathsheba's husband. I had knocked on a door and a woman said, 'Come in quickly, you might be able to help my father, he's going up the wall.' And he was, literally. He was under conviction of sin, and he kept quoting Psalm 51: 'My sin is ever before me.' He said, 'How can I be forgiven?' 'I know all about the C of E, I even know the Archbishop of Canterbury, but I am lost, a sinner with no hope.' He was acquainted with the mechanics of the ministry but not the message. The poor man was in torment until I showed him the word of peace from the Scriptures: 'My peace I give unto you...', and he began to take Christ at His word.

Sometimes I spent five hours a day knocking on doors, and it was not only difficult and even discouraging, but lonely too. Eventually I was able to visit some homes on a regular basis and a cup of tea was always welcome. There were some moments of light relief and I always looked for an opportunity to show my humour, like the day Fred and I visited the old lady who was close to the end of her life. As usual Fred read a passage and prayed a brief prayer. As we were leaving the front gate, I questioned Fred's choice of words in his prayer, 'Lord, undertake for thy servant' in the presence of someone so near to the end of her life. Fred never did that again – neither did I for that matter.

Fred and Vera Hughes lived in rented accommodation above a junk shop. In order to obtain access to their flat you had to negotiate a narrow gap through rubbish, wood full of woodworm and the smell of cat food. The old man who kept the shop, from which little seemed to be removed, had one fake ear, which he removed at night – and at other times – and placed it in splendid isolation on a table.

When Bob Otway, the candidates' secretary, visited the district with me at the end of my probation period, I made a point of taking him to Fred and Vera's flat. The flat was spotless but its location and access were quite unacceptable. There above the filthy old furniture shop, with no proper access, Fred and Vera lived without complaint. Very soon mission accommodation was provided, enabling Fred, Vera and their growing son to enjoy comparative luxury, just along the road.

Once again I was interviewed by the parent committee of the L.C.M. and was eventually accepted on to the full-time staff. It was quite exciting really, awaiting placement. A bit like being in the RAF – you went where sent, that was the theory anyway. I had my ideas too and I still wasn't inclined to go to an Anglican church; I was now a Baptist and had done with responses, confirmation and infant baptism, but I was in for a shock for the Lord had other ideas. Five weeks went by without news of a placement. It was obvious the L.C.M. didn't know what to do with me, and who could blame them? Then the letter came; it read: 'We would like you to be interviewed by a keen evangelical vicar in Islington. The Rev. J. S. Benson will see you on ... at....' Although my reservations about the Church of England were still uppermost, Joan and I felt I ought to do as asked.

When I arrived on the platform of Thornton Heath station there was one other passenger awaiting the train, my friend

Marshall Shallis, the well-known evangelist and general secretary of the Evangelization Society. 'Where are you going Lionel?' he asked. 'Oh, to see a vicar in Islington with a view to placement at his church.' 'What's his name?' 'J. S. Benson,' I replied. 'Not John Benson?' said Marshall, 'I know him, he's a close friend and a fine evangelical.' I felt ever so slightly easier and eventually reached the vicarage of Holy Trinity, Cloudesley Square, Islington. John Benson, a tall gaunt man, was waiting for me; his warm engaging smile and firm handshake were an indication of a real welcome. 'Where have you come from?' he asked. 'Thornton Heath.' 'Really?' he said, 'Do you know Marshall Shallis?' 'Yes.' I replied, 'I've just seen him at the station and he sends his greetings.' God seemed to be preparing me for something! John Benson lost no time in painting a picture of his parish and it wasn't a rosy one. He had no curate and there were 11,000 people in the parish of mixed class and race, many with 'Christian backgrounds but no backbone,' said this former Second World War army chaplain. 'I need someone to visit door-to-door,' he said, 'They need the Gospel.' I was in no doubt about the need in the parish. It wasn't going to be a picnic and I wondered what Joan would think about going to a Church of England; she had hardly set foot in one, let alone worshipped in one.

At some point John went downstairs to make coffee and bring his wife Clarissa to meet his 'prospective' colleague. While I was alone I looked around the study. There were masses of books, many by John Wesley and quite a number on Revival. Then my eyes met a bust of the great Methodist founder. What on earth was an Anglican vicar doing with a Methodist on his mantel shelf? I was to learn the answer very soon. I noticed there were some unusual worn patches on the front of the arm of the easy chair, and four more worn patches in the carpet in front of the chair. This was a mystery soon to be solved, when I learnt that John made these worn patches as he spent hours in prayer with hands holding on to the arms of the chair and with toes and knees digging into the carpet. We drank the coffee in comparative silence, after which I said, 'Vicar! I'll join you.'

I was convinced that God was sweeping aside my prejudices and, on returning home, I shared my feelings with Joan. She was receptive to these feelings. We prayed together and agreed to visit the flat offered to us by the L.C.M. in Randalls Road, Islington, above the Paget Mission Hall.

January 28 1961

It was a gloriously unseasonal sunny day as we made our way from King's Cross Station up through the back streets. 'Just a minute,' I said, this is where the coach used to go every Sunday night on the way back to Wattisham; this is where I said I would hate to live.' Now nearly six years later I was making my way up these same streets to the first real home of our own. But the flat! It was certainly spacious, but so dirty and in need of decoration.

F. H. Wrintmore, the L.C.M.'s secretary for North London, and his wife met us and showed us round the flat. 'We'll have it nice for you,' he said. Mrs Wrintmore hid her feelings well, but wasted no time in telling her husband when out of our earshot, 'You can't put that young couple in that awful flat.' Joan and I weren't exactly thrilled about it either, and we thought of the property we would have bought if I had not applied to the L.C.M. We had reached the point of no return though, and after some minor decorations to the flat, we arranged to move in. There was one problem, however; how could the removal firm get a piano up the narrow flight of stairs containing at least two sharp bends? My Bechstein upright just had to go in somehow. It did, through the second floor bedroom window. It was quite a sight, a piano suspended in mid-air and being carefully guided through the window. People came from nearby flats, some with cameras, to see and record this unusual event.

Here we were in our first home within the shadow of Victorian Beaconsfield Buildings with its landings draped in washing; water and toilet facilities were minimal and some used water from taps on the landings. For all this the people were friendly, and there was a little parade of shops at the end of Randalls Road including a general store run by two friendly, elderly Welsh ladies, who seemed to know everyone.

A new home, a new job and a new baby due in September!
Although originally I had little desire to work from an Anglican base, deep down I felt at home with the 1662 Prayer Book and the monthly, informal evening service using a supplement hymn book containing the more evangelistic hymns. The day after we moved in I did a quick tour of the parish to familiarise myself with the area, and I began to knock on doors immediately surrounding the church.

Bridge-building wasn't to be part of my evangelistic strategy; it was straight in with the Gospel, boom boom boom. 'What do you think of Jesus Christ? What about the Bible? You can't be a Christian unless you repent of sin and trust in Him.' I'd never heard of 'pre-evangelism', and the softly-softly approach hadn't occurred to me, although I was not, by nature, a confrontational person. There were a few slammed doors and choice words from affronted people, not to mention the boy who spat at me from a balcony, and I began to learn to be patient, tolerant, to accept people as they were and to be a good listener. God had given me two ears but one tongue, which might mean he wanted me to listen twice as much as speak. I was about to commence a huge learning curve that would last a long time. The people at Holy Trinity were very kind to me and showed me a great deal of warm-hearted support. There were some who didn't share my theological views but bit their lips when I was outspoken; when they responded it was often timely and helpful.

I soon became organist and choirmaster to a very acceptable choir of more than twenty singers and, to their credit, they performed anthems and oratorio choruses to a very high standard. Members lived in the locality and had to work hard to learn the music, but they enjoyed their singing and took it very seriously. Joan took over the Girl Covenanter Group and saw it grow to more than twenty in number, some of whom became committed Christians.

I kept up a disciplined programme of door-to-door visiting and, as always, was met with a mixed response. Apathy was the main barrier unless there was a crisis, and even then there was a reluctance to do anything other then 'give religion a try'. I came across some pathetic situations like the eighty-year-old man who lived in one basement room with his cat which, like him, never left it. He drank from a watering can using a tap on the landing and, until I got him a bed, he hadn't slept on one for thirty years. I was the only person allowed in, but it was worth it as we always read the Bible together and there was a rekindling of his Christian faith. Then there was the old lady who lived in a slum. Her 'pets' were three rats that she called by name.

As always the Bible played a vital part in evangelism in the parish. Arthur, a young husband, opened the door to me in Liverpool Road and told me he was looking for God now that his wife had recently been converted. I told him there was the complete answer in the Bible so that his search would not be in vain, for Deuteronomy 4:29 promises if 'you seek the Lord your God, you will find him if you look for him with all your heart and with all your soul.' He did this and, from a personal relationship with Christ, proved the Bible to be utterly reliable.

Of course the going was often tough, but one morning I was aware of the Spirit of the Lord upon me as I knocked on a door in Lonsdale Square. A young Ghanaian answered and, for once, I felt I should change my introduction. I simply said, 'I have a message from God for you.' 'In that case,' he said, 'you must come in and tell my friend as well.' Within an hour we were bowed in prayer and one of the two, Daniel, who had opened the door, came to trust in Christ as his Saviour. He and his family worshipped with us until their return to Ghana. When I returned home for lunch on that July day, Joan seemed to anticipate what I was about to tell her. She had spent considerable time that morning praying that I would be used in the conversion of just one person. No wonder I felt the Spirit of God resting on me as I visited.

All our three daughters were born during our five and a half years in Islington, Marion in September 1961, Yvonne in May 1963 and Julia in April 1966. Joan really had her hands full: there were no washing facilities, only a roof area for drying, and when it was dry, it was covered in soot from the nearby busy railway line from King's Cross.

My dear friend John Benson was patient, kind and encouraging. He knew his Bible better than anyone I've met and read it many times in a day, (including lunchtime at the Oval cricket ground during a Test match). He was a walking concordance and had memorized long passages so that he could store them up and apply them at every turn. In addition to this, he spent hours each day in prayer and his close fellowship with the Lord was evident.

North to Tottenham

It came as no surprise when, eventually, I was asked to consider a move to take over a small Mission Hall in Siddons Road, Tottenham, to which I agreed. George and Margaret Hider had worked hard there for five years and succeeded in building up a very thriving group of young people. It was a bit like jumping on a horse in full gallop. George was, and is still, an ideas man, an innovator and motivator, and it was a privilege to be asked to succeed him.

I soon set about visiting in our own street, and during my first week the Lord seemed to set his seal on the move. I arrived home after a session 'on the doors' to find an elderly gentleman at the front door. He asked to talk to me, explained that his wife was in hospital and requested that I visit her. I invited him in and he then opened his heart, telling me that he was a terrible sinner and desperately wanted to know God's forgiveness. I could tell that he was in earnest and I simply outlined God's way of salvation as contained in the Bible; he clearly understood that he needed to respond by admitting to God his sin, asking for forgiveness and trusting in God's promise to save on the grounds of Christ's death on the cross for his sin. This led to his stepson noting the change in the old man's life and he, too, came to the Mission and committed his life to the Lord, eventually becoming the Mission treasurer. So began two hectic years when our feet hardly seemed to touch the ground, but again, they were part of one huge learning curve.

5

COVENT GARDEN
AND WEST END OUTREACH

Two years in Tottenham seemed hardly long enough to make any impression on the district but in August 1968 I was asked by HQ to consider succeeding Colin Walker as missionary to West End theatres. In addition I would be expected to run the Mission Hall in Short's Gardens off Endell Street, near the former Covent Garden market, as well as reopen the ministry to the City of London Police.

I had to admit that the time spent in North London had been very eventful. Joan and I had seen much blessing. The youth and children's work continued to flourish and door-to-door visitation had brought its rewards. Old and young had responded to the Gospel and the help of a willing and competent group of co-workers proved invaluable.

In those days each missionary responsible for a hall had the privilege of the supervision of mature Christians who could act in a pastoral capacity. Mine was a Mr Ian Hill, a city businessman and a godly man who had suffered from polio and was left paralysed from the neck down. He travelled each day from Stansted via Liverpool Street to his office in the city, and twice a year I was invited to meet him. He strongly objected to the L.C.M.'s suggestion that

I move after such a short time and put his feelings in writing to my boss. Joan and I discussed the request and, of course, prayed it through. Ever supportive, Joan assured me that if I felt it right to do so then she would be happy. Disrupting the family is never easy and our eldest daughter, Marion, would be most affected as she had been settled in her junior school for two years and was making good all-round progress.

I agreed to meet Colin Walker, who was shortly due to retire, in the London Medical Mission. Colin had exercised a faithful ministry at the hall and in the theatres, and had given some time to the City of London Police. I had always admired this elder statesman of the L.C.M. but could see that he had grown tired in the work yet not tired of it. A local lady, Mary Dixie, whose walk with God was abundantly evident at every step, kept the Mission Hall in a spotless condition. She was grace personified and recommitted herself to everything the Lord required of her in support of whoever should succeed the missionary who had been in post for almost twenty years. Mary's husband, John, was one of those cockney characters who exemplified the saying 'salt of the earth'. A natural comedian, he could hold an audience with his witty reminiscences, lifting it to laughter one moment and reducing it to tears the next. Reared in Macklin Street, off Drury Lane, John Dixie rarely left the area except for a spell in the RAF during the Second World War and an annual holiday to Hope Cove. On his release from the services through sickness, he joined the Home Guard and, being a self-trained cook, spent many of his night duties frying sausages beneath Waterloo Bridge while, as he put it, 'nutting incendiary bombs into the Thames'.

While in the RAF he was converted to Christ during a guard duty in the middle of a bombing raid on an airfield in Sussex. John Dixie promised to serve God for the remainder of his life and he did just that. His public prayers were a revelation as he talked to God as a friend, though with the utmost respect. He would remind the Lord of old songs that contained some philosophical lesson relevant to his theme. When sometimes he cracked a joke to the Lord and received a rebuke from Mary, he would reply, ''e don't mind, 'e likes a joke, it keeps 'im 'appy.'

John and Mary (or Jack and Dol as they were known by some locals) had been married for more than fifty years and lived in the same two-roomed flat in Macklin Street for the whole of that time. They turned down two offers of retirement accommodation in green country pastures so that they could look after the little mission hall and its succession of London City Missionaries. John died in 1979 with the words, 'Lord, lettest now thy servant depart in peace' on his lips, and Mary slipped quietly away in 1992 in St Pancras Hospital, shortly after being visited by two of her 'boys', as she called Keith Griffiths and me.

The L.C.M. has had a presence in the Seven Dials area since the birth of the London City Mission in 1835, and I was proud to be considered suitable to follow in the footsteps of my illustrious predecessors. The London Medical Mission came into L.C.M. hands soon after the birth of the National Health Service in 1948. My induction took place on 14 October 1968. The small room upstairs used as a meeting place was full on that Monday evening with friends and well-wishers. F. H. Wrintmore, my immediate 'boss', presided and preached the sermon based on the words of the apostle Paul in Acts 27:25: 'I believe God for it shall be even as it was told me.' These were encouraging words to a young missionary whose ministry was to be centred in the heart of Soho with its sordid dives, nightclubs, sex shops, brothels and blocks of flats.

The following Sunday at 6 p.m. found me standing to address seven elderly people plus Joan and our three girls. This was in contrast to six days earlier when the hall at Tottenham was full for our farewell meeting. I knew that things could change although it would require God's hand to do it. My first sermon was based on

Gideon's experience in Judges 6, during which God showed him what he could do with a diminished army. I visualised the hall full of people and believed that it would happen, provided I was obedient. That wasn't all; there were theatre managers to be visited and permission to be granted for regular calls upon backstage and front-of-house staff. As the weeks went by our Sunday evening numbers increased and we were joined by two young medical students training at Guy's Hospital, who were anxious to do some door-to-door visitation or be involved in any 'hands on' evangelism!

Nigel Jones and Elizabeth Hogwood met me every Monday evening and together we knocked on the doors of the surrounding blocks of flats off Drury Lane. Nigel and Liz were a tremendous encouragement with their youthful evangelistic zeal and anything they put their minds and hands to they did with all their might. They married the following year, subsequently making their mark in the medical world as well as influencing many for Christ in London and other parts of England.

Whenever I hear the wail of the Coronation Street signature tune, I am reminded of the times I heard it on the other side of doors at which we knocked. Little did I realise just how unpopular we were through interrupting an episode in the lives of Ken Barlow, Annie Walker and Ena Sharples, and there were no video recorders in those days which could be used as a back-up should the doorbell or telephone ring. I joined the London City Mission aware of the fact that house-to-house visitation was the bread and butter of its many evangelistic opportunities. It is probably the most difficult aspect of the work of evangelism and constitutes a real challenge, but as soon as the door is opened and the initial pleasantries, from my side anyway, are exchanged, the sense of fear and apprehension begins to disappear. Blocks of flats always presented me with more psychological and physical difficulty than street dwellings. Their very size, often ten floors and more, with scores of steps to climb, was forbidding. I always began at the top but don't ask me why; maybe it was the feeling that having begun at the highest number, I was on my way home so to speak.

I find people interesting and this enables me to cope with those who have no desire to accept my message even if they are confrontational and even rude. Provided the door remains open then I can be patient enough to face and counter opposition. 'Get people talking' has always been my maxim, be a good listener, discover where they are coming from and don't register shock at anything they say. People must be accepted as they are and their opinions, theories, philosophies and experiences are obviously important to them, so let them air them. By the same token my opinions are equally important; no one can gainsay my experiences. Above all the Bible is God's truth and, as a minister of His Gospel, I have the right to make it known graciously, yet firmly and with authority. I must, in the words of the apostle Peter, 'Always be prepared to give an answer to everyone who asks you to give the reason for the hope that you have. But do this with gentleness and respect...' (1 Peter 3:15).

I learned the nursery rhyme 'Have you seen the muffin man who lives in Drury Lane' as a child and here I was visiting blocks of flats off that very street in central London. There is no longer a muffin man in Drury Lane, it's just a busy thoroughfare used as a cut-through for traffic between the Aldwych and New Oxford Street. Each session of visits brought me into contact with at least one interesting and worthwhile contact. There was the sixty-year-old man who invited Nigel and me into his living room. It was filled with the largest bed I had ever seen. It soon became evident that his lifestyle was one of gross immorality. The little two-roomed dwelling was being used as a brothel and he was living off the earnings of 'his' girls. As he had some knowledge of the Bible it was easy to reason with him and point out the error of his ways. He produced a large family Bible and I turned to some relevant passages: 'Though your sins be as scarlet, they shall be as white as snow; though they be red like crimson, they shall be as wool', 'If you will be willing and obedient...', were among the Scriptures we read and whose promises we trusted. We felt the presence of evil in that little flat, yet as we knelt at the bedside at his request, to know forgiveness, God's Spirit had begun His cleansing work.

Door-to-door visiting reaps very little reward if you don't have a strategy and a follow-up programme. Evening visits ensure more people are contacted and you are more likely to meet the menfolk. These days, however, people are less inclined to open their doors on winter evenings so summer evenings are favourite. Questionnaires are very useful and can be left with people for collection and contact at a later date, but the visitor with a good mental stock of questions likely to be asked can achieve much there and then. The sooner you get graciously to the point the better. Almost every person you meet has a point of view about religion or Christianity; find out what it is (you may learn something), listen and respond but 'keep the door open' for next time. Show genuine interest in the other person and, without prying, discover something about them, their interests, family situation and background, and next time round you'll have points of contact.

Just off Drury Lane is a little street called Macklin Street. I knocked at the door of one of the small almshouses tucked away in its own courtyard. An elderly lady answered my knock and obviously thought I was the gasman. I assured her otherwise before I went in so that she felt safe with a stranger. Amy Cunard was one of the original Tiller Girls, a famous team of dancers, and her late husband, Jock Cunard, was a member of the equally famous music hall clog-dancing act the 'Eight Lancashire Lads'. Before marrying Jock, Amy had been engaged to Albert Whelan, famous for making his stage entrance immaculately turned out in evening dress, whistling his signature tune 'The Jolly Brothers', while he casually removed his white gloves, white scarf and top hat and handed them, together with his cane, to a stage assistant. I had seen Albert Whelan on stage, so on subsequent visits I whistled his signature tune as I heard Amy shuffling to the closed door. Her eyes lit up and she broke into a smile as she opened the door. This was my point of contact for future visits. I would knock on her door, wait for the sound of her shuffling along the passage – contrast this with her high kicking can-can days with the Tiller Girls – and I would whistle the 'Jolly Brothers'. The door would open and Amy would say, 'Ah, it's Albert, come in Albert.' Amy remembered those days in show business, touring the country from theatre to theatre, for many reasons, not least for the chaplain's visits. By this time I had begun to look for openings in some of the theatres, and Amy assured me of the desperate need for someone like me to visit backstage areas, read the Bible and acquaint members of the profession with God. Amy loved the Bible, and I would read to her and pray with her; and I had the joy of pointing her along the way of salvation.

I had to admit that trying to cope with a ministry at a mission hall (now called Christian centres), contact theatre employees and visit the City Police Service was a very tall order. There was always the danger of spreading myself too thinly and lessening the effect in all three areas. However, the opportunities were there and I determined to establish a presence, and trust that help at the hall would come eventually.

Within the first three months our little hall became the scene of a lively Sunday evening meeting. From an average congregation of twelve, we were now seeing thirty, some of whom had not been inside a church for many years. The Bible was at the centre of our ministry, and Joan and I firmly believed that it could speak to any generation and in any situation. We brought the Sunday evening meeting from the upper room, always considered to be the chapel, to the ground floor where we were literally at street level and could actually 'reach out' and invite people in. For twenty minutes before each meeting we would do this and it often worked. I delivered 500 personal invitations around the district, welcoming people to our meetings, and the response was good. An Ethiopian man in his fifties asked for a visit. I found him in utter squalor and set about helping him in a practical way. He came to the hall, responded to the Gospel and became a keen student of the Bible.

Joan contacted a lady as she passed the hall one Sunday evening; she came in and was restored to faith in God, having been a backslider for many years.

I contacted people, young and old, wherever I could, in their homes, in the shops and on the streets. Once, a group of a dozen youngsters barricaded themselves in a disused school in Endell Street. The police were called but failed to eject them and the neighbours were angry. I contacted the police, asking if I could do anything and was told I hadn't a hope of getting them out. One afternoon I knocked hard on the side door of the old school; it opened to about two inches and a voice asked, 'Is it the law?' 'No!' I replied, 'I'm from the Mission Hall and I would like to talk to you and invite you to come round for a meal this afternoon.' I was invited inside and joined about a dozen young people of both sexes and a couple of dogs in a darkened basement room. After drinking the dirty mug of tea I was offered, I told them that there would be a meal of fish and chips available within the hour if they cared to come to the mission. They agreed without question, and the faithful Mary Dixie prepared the table and collected the fare from the shop while I sat with them and talked about Christian matters. I reasoned with them about their lifestyle, explaining why it is so unsociable to take over a building that was needed for public use. One of them had with him a guitar, so I played the piano and together we went through a repertoire of familiar songs and hymns, including 'Amazing Grace'. Picture the scene, me in my neat suit and collar and tie, surrounded by a group of hippies complete with all the gear, explaining the wonder of God's Grace as in the life of John Newton, the writer of the words we had just been singing.

The following day, two of the young people sought me out, one of them a young girl of fourteen who had absconded from a children's home in the West Country. I contacted the matron, who was thrilled to know the runaway had been found, and I put the girl on the train within hours.

Some days later a letter arrived from the young girl thanking me for my help in rescuing her from a life of sex, drugs and alcohol, and, she said, 'Telling me about Jesus.'

Did the group vacate the building? Yes they did, the next day, and I had the privilege (pleasure) of informing the police that it was as easy as that.

A friend of mine, John Hester, had written a book about his ministry at St Anne's Soho, entitled appropriately *Soho is My Parish*, in which he related many stories of people he had helped. John was a great inspiration to me and gave me an insight into many aspects of the sordid side of life in the area. I know that both he and Joan, my wife, and the Dixies prayed daily for me, and how I needed it, for I was as green as the proverbial grass and naïve with it too. Protection was what I needed, physical, mental and spiritual covering, as I made visits in Old and New Compton Streets, Beak Street, Windmill Street, Rupert Street, Lisle Street and a host of little courtyards and alleyways. I would go with my literature to the nightclubs and strip joints, the pornography shops and the cinemas where only the most sordid films were shown. In most cases I got no further than the door and spent time talking to the receptionist.

Often I would be there at the request of a relative (usually a mother) living out in the country, whose son or daughter of fourteen or fifteen had left home and decided to 'hide away' in London. Armed with a photograph or letter I went from club to club asking, 'Have you seen this person?' Amazingly I would often be put in touch with the youngsters and incur the wrath of the proprietor or pimp, as I reasoned with the prodigal. The devil is no respecter of persons or upbringing, and sometimes I would be looking for the teenage member of a Christian family who had been lured away in the wrong company. Distraught parents, who had prayed for their child since birth and whose prayers appeared to be in vain, would ring daily to see if there was any news.

My colleague and friend Keith Griffiths visited with me in a nightclub off D'Arblay Street at the request of a distraught mother living in Bristol, whose fourteen-year-old son had disappeared. Within days following our initial visit, I found him working in a brothel. I happened to visit the owner of a sordid dive in one of the side streets who told me over coffee that he had been brought up in a Christian environment and for fourteen years had read his Bible using Scripture Union Bible notes. He had been enticed into Soho's gay scene and was in the business of picking up rent boys off the streets for immoral purposes. Yes, he knew the lad I was looking for; he had recently been 'picked up'. There was a happy reunion in that Christian home in Bristol not many days later.

Of course Soho is not all about nightlife; it's going on in the daytime too. Once a week I would visit the strip club doors during the lunchtime and, although I would be distracting the staff from doing business had I been allowed in, I often spoke to the receptionists and doorkeepers. 'God made sex so he must have wanted us to enjoy it,' I would be told. 'Do you really enjoy what you are doing?' I would ask. The answer was always, 'No! But we get paid for it and we need the money so we are prepared to risk all the dangers involved.' Although I would put all the theological, moral, physical and biological arguments against such a profession, nothing could happen without the convicting and life-changing work of the Holy Spirit.

Somehow Elaine gave the impression of being not exactly under conviction, but most certainly feeling conscience-stricken each time I called. As she admitted well-dressed men in their thirties and forties to one of the most notorious peep show establishments in Soho, she was always interested to hear what I had to say. Hers was a costly business because it was a dirty business, and her face bore the marks of past experiences. I sowed a lot of seed in her mind and, I trust, in her heart. She didn't seem to mind 'her girls' knowing who I was or that she held regular conversations with me. Elaine would commute into London looking much like any other young woman her age; no-one would have any idea what profession occupied her day or night, yet was she any harder to reach than anyone else? Most definitely not; 'with God nothing is impossible.' There were those who were even harder to reach who regularly attended churches within a stone's throw of the place where we were standing. I knew the truth of Ephesians 6:12: 'We wrestle not against flesh and blood, but against principalities, against powers, against the rulers of the darkness of this world, against spiritual wickedness in high places.' (KJV) I was to experience only too well the reality of the verse in the days to come.

Recalling a visit to the former Windmill Theatre, which stood by its famous motto 'We never close' and where scores of well-known artistes stepped on to the first rung of the showbusiness ladder, I met a Russian arm-wrestler. A champion in his home country, he would take on all-comers between erotic dances on stage. 'I'm a wrestler too.' I said during our introduction. He laughed as he eyed my slight figure up and down and noticed my slim fingers, which were more at home on the keyboard than grappling with the great fists of a fifteen-stone all-muscle Russian. 'You a wrestler?' he quizzed. 'Yes,' I said, 'an all-in wrestler, who doesn't wrestle against flesh but against spiritual wickedness, one who has to be aware of every spiritual dirty trick in the devil's armoury. No amount of physical training and expertise can prepare you to cope with the strength and subtlety of the devil,' I told him. 'I can introduce you to Jesus Christ who will release you from sin and give you an inner strength.' This was a message he had never heard, having been brought up under the atheistic dogma of communism.

I have already referred to the ministry of finding missing persons in Soho but can recall one case of this nature which took me further afield. The work of the Salvation Army among missing persons is known worldwide and they enjoy some success. Such a ministry is specialized and requires not only training, background knowledge of the subjects and whom to contact, but dedication, a reliance on prayer, sensitivity and wisdom. Although I had a limited amount of experience in this kind of work, I wasn't as equipped as I might be; and I didn't consider, with my other commitments, that I could cope with something so time-consuming except as the occasion arose.

However, such an occasion did arise when a young wife, not known to me, was given my telephone number and rang me one Sunday afternoon. Her husband had walked out on her and the two young children ten days before, and there was no trace of him. The police had been alerted but there was no news. I hurried off to the flat in east London to find the distressed wife and children fearing that he had committed suicide. What could I do? I telephoned Joan and asked her to pray and look after the evening service at the mission. She prayed that the wife might find some comfort from the Bible and I sought to bring some support to the family. I gathered them around and we knelt to pray. 'Lord,' I prayed, 'You know exactly where Alan is now, please arrest him, deal with his conscience and compel him to telephone his wife immediately.' This was at approximately six o'clock. I left the home and made my way to the West End, arriving as the service was ending. On my arrival home the telephone rang. It was the overjoyed young wife informing me that her husband had been found and had telephoned. At approximately six o'clock, even as we were praying, a young man was handing out invitations to attend a church service and came across Alan on the seafront at

Southend. They talked, and it was suggested Alan telephone his wife immediately which he did. The young man was given my telephone number and got in touch, telling me that he would give Alan a bed for the night and could bring him to meet me the next day. When I called for his wife the next day, she told me she had found comfort in the Scriptures and was assured something would happen soon.

I cannot forget the thrill of seeing these two reunited, as arranged, at a point near Gallows Corner on the A12. I drove them to their home and witnessed the sheer emotion and gratitude of the two children as they ran in from school to find daddy safely home once again. That was only the beginning; there was much rethinking, planning and patience, and many practical issues to be considered before the family could once again become stable.

Psalm 127:1 makes the clear observation that 'except the Lord build the house, they labour in vain that build it.'(KJV) This applies to family life, but all buildings require constant attention and maintenance if they are to survive the rigorous storms and experiences of life. The couple referred to had been heavily involved in Christian work, but such involvement does not always ensure protection against the breakdown of the family unit, unless its members work together in order to prevent the devil from driving a wedge between them. A Christian friend of mine was travelling on a train when he was aware of the young man in the opposite seat bowing in an attitude of prayer. My friend took the opportunity of speaking to him, asking him about his Christian beliefs. 'Oh, I'm not a Christian,' he replied, 'This is the hour and the day when all members of occult groups are urged to pray for the breakdown of Christian marriages.' What a challenge this is to all Christians, to regularly pray for the protection of relationships within Christian family life. Moreover, what about the need to bring to God in prayer the marriages of Christian ministers and missionaries where, we are told, breakdowns are on the increase?

As a young Christian I often heard it said, 'The family that prays together stays together' and many have proved this true, but I am sure there are also those who say, 'It didn't work for us'. Each case has to be considered within its context, and parties have to work at the relationship in order to achieve any measure of success.

Joan and I were always aware that anything we were able to do was barely scratching the surface, as the task of just sowing seeds and bearing fruit was immense. Drug addiction had become an increasing problem in London, and the streets of Soho were alive with drug peddlers and those who lived from one fix to the next.

Although we were seeing increased attendance on Sunday evenings, apart from the faithful efforts of a group of National Young Life Campaigners who worked weekly among children, very little was being done for people on the streets. Early in 1971 we put the facts to the Lord in prayer: 'Lord we want to reach outsiders, bring them in and see them converted to Christ. We have the premises but we need people to help us.' Throughout our married life we have, whenever possible, read the Scriptures and prayed together. We had the witness in our spirit that our prayers would be answered and things moved very quickly.

Sandy Millar, now a Bishop, and formerly the much blessed-by-God vicar of Holy Trinity, Brompton, then a young barrister, and his friend Rod Haswell were walking through Short's Gardens near Covent Garden Station, searching for premises into which they could invite those who were addicted to drugs and alcohol. They saw the open door of the Mission Hall, went in and found no one who could help them except, that is, a copy of the London City Mission magazine. Filled with the certainty that if anyone would be willing to help it would be the L.C.M., Sandy telephoned headquarters and Stanley Turner gave him my telephone number. Sandy and I met that day. He assured me he could raise a team of volunteers linked with the Steward's Trust and attending Holy Trinity, Brompton; we agreed to meet on an early date, complete with team, to pray and plan. Our vision was the same, even though we had not met before, and God quickly sealed His plan for us.

Seventeen of us – ages varying between twenty and sixty – would meet to worship God, hear the Scriptures, pray and set out a simple strategy for our first outreach. March 18 was the date set. Half the team would pray at the mission while the other half would go out in two's on to the streets and invite people in. Those who came in would be fed first, and none would leave without hearing of the claims of Christ. Those who would not accept the invitation would still be presented with the Gospel. It was a simple scriptural strategy based on the Lord's commission to 'Go out into the highways and byways and compel them to come in'. Strangely enough we never even considered training sessions, even though less than half of us could claim any experience in this kind of evangelism. This was particularly awesome for me as I had been elected team leader of a group of people most of whom held responsible positions in business. There was no desire by Sandy, or any team member, to 'take over' and we were to be 'labourers together with God'.

With the exception of four of us, the team was very young in the Christian faith and consisted of secretaries, nurses, teachers, housewives, a lawyer, a banker and others in professional life. Vic Ramsey, who had worked for some years in the drug scene and had seen numbers rehabilitated and converted to the Christian faith, offered this advice: 'Expect some disappointments.' This was telling us to keep our feet on the ground and face up to all the realities of such a ministry. Work among drug addicts in the seventies was a sort of bandwagon upon which numbers of people in their first flush of conversion to Christ would climb. Some relied heavily upon their own experiences and were not too conversant with the Bible, and when they did use the Scriptures they were often taken out of context. Consequently when the going was hard and discouragement came, their commitment waned and the work suffered. No one was actually invited to join our team, for we relied solely upon those sent by God who possessed a clear call and a determination to be good, reliable and accountable team members. There were a few simple rules for each team member: spend time in prayer, especially on the Thursday of the outreach, commit yourself to being present each week, be on time and stay until closing time at 10.30 p.m. Counselling was to be done within the context of the meeting, and male and female were not to meet privately. Sandy or I were to be made aware of situations and there would be monthly team meetings where we could worship, pray through and discuss issues and strategy.

The names of those team members who were at our first meeting come quickly to mind and they were very special. There was Rodney Radcliffe, Anthony Turner, Charles Cordle, Nicholas Rivett-Carnac, Helen Clark, Mary Bird, Peggy Stevens, Annette Fisher (who that year married Sandy), Diana Quicke, Jenny (I can't recall the surname), Dorothy Kerr and of course, Sandy. Soon we would be joined by other stalwarts like Marigold Copeland (who married Nicholas), Judy (who married Rodney), and Nigel Cumming who met Liz, another team member, and married her, subsequently entering the Anglican ministry. There were also Anne Burnell, Margaret Driskell, Hazel Bryant, and Colin Greenwood who was assigned to the team by the London City Mission. John Phillips became the first team member who initially came in from the streets, responded to the Gospel and became a regular worker.

On the first evening eight young people were fished in. We welcomed them, fed them and sang two choruses which summed up the convictions of all of us, 'Only believe, all things are possible, only believe' and 'His name is wonderful'. I gave a brief talk on a verse from the Bible, and the team members who had been sitting alongside our visitors began to talk to them. Remember that the lifestyles of the team members were a long way from those who had become used to street life, so how could they possibly relate and cross such a wide gulf? Firstly, they were good listeners and non-patronising. They were gracious in manner and took any rebuff with a soft answer. They showed a tremendous sense of love and concern and, above all, they were supported by prayer and filled with the Holy Spirit and the conviction that He would compensate for any inadequacy they had.

Did I say inadequacy? Well, this was me, and here I must testify to the blessing I received through working with such a team of Spirit-filled Christians. They not only spoke convincingly of the filling of the Spirit but exemplified this in their conversation and behaviour. I saw the need to open myself up to God and let His Spirit take full control and make me adequate to the task of seeing people and situations changed and lives won for Christ. 'I will pour water upon him that is thirsty and floods upon the dry ground', I read in Isaiah 44:3 (KJV); and in the margin of my old Bible, opposite the verse, I had written, 'Please God'. Joan will testify to similar experiences based on Scripture and helped by members of the team who prayed for and with us. I saw any experience of the touch of God's Holy Spirit on my life not as a 'one-off' but as a continuous act of God's Grace and blessing bestowed on me for effective service, and not for my own self-gratification. God answered my prayer, kept His promise and touched my life, not just once but many times since. During these West End days, I was never more conscious of the spiritual warfare than when I was seeing God at work in the lives of those with whom I had contact. Ephesians 6:11, with its emphasis on the whole armour of God as being the complete answer to all the wiles of the devil, became totally relevant.

Returning to that first night of West End Outreach, God put His seal on the proceedings when, subsequently, one of those who were brought in responded to Christ's claim to his life and kicked the drug habit, left the scene, returned home and linked with his local church. So began what has been recognized by all who saw anything of this work, a unique period in the history of evangelism in that particular part of London. Within weeks there was no need to go out each evening fishing for young people as word of mouth was sufficient to add to our numbers, and each week we would see a crowd of between sixty and seventy present. The London Medical Mission (still bearing the name it was given in 1872) became known on the streets of Soho and Covent Garden as 'The London Miracle Mission'. Unlike many Christian outreach centres, we fed them first rather than subject them to a so-called 'God-spot' before opening the food hatch. We believed that the Lord would keep those in the hall whom He wanted after the 'loaves and fishes' had been distributed, and only occasionally did anyone leave. Those who came in from the streets saw in the team 'Christ in action'. There was real harmony in the team, and this showed itself at all times to people who were surprisingly discerning and would have been quick to react had there been the slightest note of disharmony. For my part, I found myself able to work alongside Christians who didn't always dot every evangelical 'i' and cross every evangelical 't', but who showed a real commitment to Christ and a love for those both inside and outside the Kingdom.

Singing was always a feature of the evening and attracted numbers of new people. In the summer, windows and doors were opened and the sound of music could be heard in Shorts Gardens, Endell Street and Neal Street. It wasn't a raucous noise as you might hear in a nearby pub, but in many cases came out of sincere hearts with every word meant. We compiled our own songbook and included some of the new choruses as well as the old and more familiar hymns. There was always a twenty-minute (sometimes longer) talk, and with very few exceptions this was listened to in complete silence.

One evening a formidable looking gang, who appeared to adopt a threatening attitude, visited us. They sat through the evening and as we were about to close, one of them came up to me and told me that he and his mates had been responsible for breaking up a number of meetings such as ours and this was their intention this evening. When I asked him why it didn't happen here he replied, 'Because we couldn't, there's a power here we couldn't break down, a kind of atmosphere'. It wasn't the only time this was to happen. A couple of young men who came in one evening had been involved with probably the most notorious East End gang, the Krays. They recognized some of the clientele as ex-prisoners and, becoming concerned for my safety, one of them offered himself as my bodyguard, telling me that some of those in the hall that evening were dangerous. He came for many weeks and on one occasion was very moved by the power of the evening. No-one dared speak when I was speaking or Nick would threaten them with 'a bunch of knuckles'. We didn't require that kind of protection but appreciated his concern.

One evening during the summer when all the doors were open and the singing in progress, a drunk came in carrying a large flagon of cider. We had a strict rule that bottles of alcohol were not to be brought into the hall, but we could do little about that which was already consumed unless the possessor became violent. He sat in the front and I was aware of the possibility of a difficult situation arising, so I prayed that he might go as quickly as he came without disruption. I had hardly stopped praying when a powerful looking individual came to the door and without so much as a 'by your leave' came in, picked up the offending container and marched off with it, followed quickly by a protesting owner.

On another occasion, during a particularly sensitive time in the proceedings, a drugged-up individual, with whom we had spent a lot of time and for whom a great deal of prayer had been offered, came in looking extremely vicious and bent on causing trouble. He began to swear and blaspheme the name of Christ and then proceeded to lift the piano as if to turn it over. I tried to reason with him but he turned against me with the most vile language.

Up got a tough-looking individual, known on the drug scene as 'Daddy Tony', and took the offender in a vice-like grip, pinned him against the wall and told him that his language and behaviour were offensive and that he would not sit and hear the name of Jesus defiled by profane lips. He then frogmarched him from the room and into the street with the warning to stay clear of the building in future. He did return, but to apologize for his behaviour. I received a very touching card from him on my retirement, which I greatly appreciated.

Thankfully these situations were the exception, and on no occasion did we have to call in the police; although they were well aware of our activities, they never came looking for wanted persons or were to be seen in the vicinity on Thursday evenings. We were always mindful of the protection of God, as indeed I was when one man insisted he have a private conversation with me in my office and was as close as at any time to using a knife on me. I had quickly asked my faithful colleague, fourteen stone, six foot, Colin Greenwood, to stand close to the door just in case, although there was little he could have done against the quick flash of a six-inch knife should it be used. The problem was caused when a team member broke the rules and became too friendly with the man, and when I stepped in I became his target. The girl, a keen Christian, had been totally taken in by the married man's persuasive attentions and they announced to me that 'the Lord wanted them to be together'.

How lightly and selfishly even Christians hold the Lord's name, and what strange things He appears to 'tell' them to do. Taking the Lord's name in vain covers more than using His name as a swear word and renders those who use it guilty. Sometimes to many people in Christian circles 'The Lord told me' is another way of saying, 'This is what I want.' God's will is seldom easy to discern and almost invariably depends on three things: facts, faith and feelings. This includes prayer, the Bible, circumstances and the advice of friends or fellowship before we can begin to consider it as His will. On the other hand it often requires plain, good, old-fashioned common sense. This particular situation was resolved, but only after I, with the team's agreement, took the young lady off the team, gave her counsel in the presence of another lady, prayed with her and eventually was assured that the relationship had ended.

Those Thursday evenings were full of surprises. One young man came in dressed in long robes and sandals, wearing a beard and long hair. 'I'm Jesus Christ,' he proclaimed, as I looked at him without registering an expression of shock. 'Are you?' I replied. 'You don't believe me, do you?' he said. 'Then will you show me your hands?' I asked. He did, and I shook my head, 'I don't see the marks of the nails on your hands,' I told him, 'so you can't possibly be my Lord Jesus Christ.' He refused to be convinced.

I was sitting next to another young man one evening and asked him where he was born. 'Even if I told you, you wouldn't know the place,' he said. 'Try me,' I said. 'Kington,' he said. 'What's your name?' I asked him. He told me his name and I recognized it. 'Do you have an Uncle Cliff?' I asked. 'Yes I do,' he replied. You should have seen his face when I told him that I was born near Kington and his uncle used to deliver meat to our door every week.

They came from everywhere and out of every background, on to the streets of London and into the little Mission Hall where there was a welcome for all.

There was the man who came under conviction and broke down in tears when I spoke about 'the heart being deceitful above all things and desperately wicked' (Jer. 17:9). 'I know, I know,' he sobbed, 'I've preached from that verse, I was a minister of the Gospel.' Then there was Clive who had been a captain in the army, then a public schoolmaster, and whose father was a High Court Judge. Alcohol had been his downfall and he took to the streets. He was ever the gentleman in manner and speech and spent his days in the library. One night after our meeting he knelt in prayer and submission to God as he trusted Christ as His Saviour.

Two rival groups, both addicted to drugs and alcohol, were present one evening. During the singing they became involved in some intimidating crosstalk. Team members began to pray and a potentially nasty situation was defused. Afterwards I took Ronnie, one of the ringleaders, aside and began to talk with him. His appearance, through years of loose living and alcohol, gave the lie to his age of thirty-three. Ronnie told me that he was sleeping in a derelict house when a fire broke out and mercifully he woke just in time. Nearby he found a jacket as he fled the building and, when he searched the pockets, he found a booklet entitled 'Fear Not' with the Mission Hall stamp on it. Now Ronnie was pouring out his soul to me, and as he did so he was sobering up. Coming from a Protestant background in Ireland, he remembered so much of what he had learned. Bible stories and hymns from those happy days were reward to him now and we sang his favourite, 'O Love, that wilt not let me go'. Ronnie was expressing just how true that was for him.

I think of another Ronnie who one evening came and approached me saying he felt he was in bondage to drug abuse. 'I desperately want to be freed, please help me,' he said. I gathered three other team members around me, and we listened to Ronnie as he convinced us he was in earnest about kicking his habit. He had been involved in occult activities and, although not too deeply, we knew we were likely to be out of our depth. We prayed and read the Scriptures and claimed their power and promises. 'The blood of Jesus Christ cleanses from all sin' (1 John 1:7) was one of the many we read. We asked the Lord to protect us as we wrestled against the dark powers of the air and unseen wickedness. We prayed for Ronnie's release from bondage, but he had to respond, which he did, confessing sin and trusting in the finished work of Christ who died on the cross. He said, 'I'm free, and I feel as if a burden has been lifted from me.' I witnessed the destruction of his drugs and syringes and saw him write a letter requesting admission to a rehabilitation centre. He was accepted and stayed the course in spite of one lapse, and, although he moved away, he kept in touch. Some months later I was speaking at a church meeting on the south coast. During my address I referred to Ronnie, though not by name, and at the close of the meeting the chairman, showing a measure of excitement, told us that a young man fitting Ronnie's description had been contacting young people on the seafront, telling them about Christ and bringing them to the church. There was no doubt who the young man was.

The old Sankey Hymn Book contains a number of what are considered to be sentimental stories of prodigals who forsake home and family for the 'pleasures of sin', and inevitably there was the old mother who prayed with tears for her child's return. Don't deride such stories; I've seen such things happen in reality as in the case of Alan.

Alan left his home in Scotland and joined the Navy but was dishonourably discharged. The problem? Alcohol. For years he lived on the streets of London, and his lifestyle made him look older than his forty years. He came into the mission one Sunday and on a succession of Sundays, taking an interest in the Bible. One Sunday evening I based my sermon on Romans 5:6. 'When we were without strength Christ died for the ungodly'. 'That's for me,' said Alan, 'I haven't got the strength to cope with my alcoholism but I believe Christ has.' He responded immediately, as I preached, and determined to follow Christ. Within days he had returned to Scotland, found his old mother in a home and their reunion was beyond words. 'I've been praying for you for years,' she said through her tears, 'and now you've come.' The Bible reminds us that 'the way of the transgressor is hard'; Alan proved this as he struggled to stay sober and straight, although he received thorough follow-up and rehabilitation. Often these old hymns of experience don't tell the whole story.

Travel to Covent Garden Station, walk along Neal Street and on the right hand side you will see 'Café Eterno. It stands on the site of the old Mission Hall where so many of the happenings I've related occurred. Café Eterno is just part of the London City Mission's work in a multi-ministry centre and provides opportunity for acquainting people of all nations and backgrounds with the Christian Gospel. I was privileged to recount, at the building's opening ceremony in 1998, the L.C.M.'s involvement in the area over 163 years.

Seated in the audience was John Phillips who came inside the old hall to one of our early outreach meetings. Tired and hungry, he was only interested in the food and shelter, and when approached by a team member who spoke about Jesus Christ, John's response was a terse 'Get lost!' John approached me on a subsequent Thursday evening and asked if I might get him a pair of shoes as he was to be interviewed for a job the following week. I said I would do my best and suggested he came back the following Sunday. I cannot recall how I came about the new pair of shoes but they were available on the Sunday and John was there to collect them. He got the job and continued to come to the meetings. One evening John came through to faith in Christ and became a team member. I managed to help him obtain more permanent employment, since when he has not only bettered himself but is a small shareholder in the firm. With his brilliant mind for figures John regularly checked my Mission accounts and never made a mistake. I used to work them out with a calculator and John would speed check them correctly. In a recent letter John refers to those days of blessing as being 'unique', and considers the caring ministry of the team to have been one of its great strengths.

'All things are possible, only believe', we sang in those early days of West End Outreach, and many a broken life was repaired through the power of Christ. Like Bruce who had been an apprentice jockey but was sacked as he was considered a security risk. He turned to thieving, and could walk into M & S, change from rags into new and fashionable clothes and walk out without being detected. He would steal a week's food from a supermarket without it being missed. 'I could get you

With drug users on Eros in Piccadilly Circus †

a brand new gold cross for your mission,' he once told me. After two hours of wrestling with his soul he announced to Sandy Millar and me that he was 'turning his back' on God. We watched him disappear into the murky streets of Seven Dials and prayed God would arrest him, which He did. A keen Christian worker found Bruce in a derelict house in Glasgow and he was cornered by the same Gospel he had heard in the London City Mission Hall. He gave in and one evening, as I bowed in prayer at my table just inside the open door, he crept in. When I opened my eyes there was Bruce. 'Remember me?' he asked. I said, 'Yes, the jockey stealing the gold cross and, most vivid of all, "I'm turning my back on God". It's Bruce,' I said. 'Yes,' he said, 'I'm going to confess to the police and pay back all I owe to whoever I owe money.' He had written a list and proved true to his word. And the police? Well, they were completely taken aback but did no more about it. Bruce saved enough money to take himself through Bible college and he and his wife made their home in Scotland.

What did Vic Ramsey say? 'Expect disappointments'. He was right and there were many, very many. Like Black Magic Billy and Dave, Den and Eddy, Mick, and dear old Ratso who loved the Mission really and sent me a card on my retirement. There were those who did further time in prison; one was sent down for murder. I remember tracing him to a hospital where he was barely conscious. He awoke to find me praying at the foot of his bed and broke down in tears. Sadly he became an alcoholic and his brain deadened. Once, when he saw me some years later, he was so befuddled that all he could say was, 'Piano, piano' as he remembered me playing the piano in the Mission Hall on those exciting Thursday evenings. There will, in spite of many disappointments, be many surprises in heaven, for our God is the God of surprises.

I have often been asked what was the secret of such a ministry but have not put my finger on it, although I would like to quote Nicholas Rivett-Carnac who was a member of the original team:

> I believe that the unity, love and mutual respect that the Lord gave us for each other and each other's ministries played a large part in enabling the Holy Spirit to be released so wonderfully among us. It was inspiring to see the team rushing to get there and going straight up to the 'upper room' to pray without having had anything to eat or drink. Those pre-meeting prayers were powerful. The praise and worship led by you and Sandy were under the beautiful anointing and we always enjoyed the ministry of the Word. It was a privilege to welcome so many needy and hurting people to the London City Mission Hall, and I believe that they were all met with such loving acceptance that they must **all** have been helped in some way or another, and they certainly enjoyed the refreshments provided by willing helpers. Love was in the air and more than two or three romances developed between helpers. More was happening between Marigold and me than we realised and certainly between Sandy and Annette. I remember being there one Christmas Day when a number of visitors gave their lives to the Lord as, of course, some did on the Thursday evenings – Praise the Lord.

Rodney Radcliffe remembers clearly the warm, welcoming non-threatening attitude of the team towards those who came into

the Mission, and yet there was a discernment and spiritual understanding of the needs they faced. Many of us had little or no
training in dealing with those who were heavily addicted to drugs
and alcohol or possessed by demons, and we were sometimes out
of our depth, but we learned and leaned heavily on the Lord and
the guidance of His Spirit.

That old brick building was the place of miracles and we are
grateful for its legacy; for the godly doctors and nurses who served
in its medical days prior to the birth of the National Health Service
in 1948; for the Basden family from Northwood who financed
its structure in the 1930s; for the Dixies and their loyalty and
simple faith in the God who never fails; for Joan and our three
girls, Marion, Yvonne and Julia who, as very young children, grew
up in the work and were with us each Sunday evening for eight
and a half years, serving food and often accompanying the singing.
The family now needed the security of church family near our
home rather than divided loyalties. I needed to concentrate on the
growing opportunities in theatres as well as the City of London
Police, so I asked the L.C.M. if they would consider replacing
me at the Mission Hall. This they did, and we said farewell to
a crowded Mission of friends, many of whom testified to God's
blessing upon their lives.

6

WEST END THEATRES

Just picture the scene in a dressing room in one of London's
theatres. A group of ten or twelve young people sat with their
Bibles open, eagerly discussing the appointed passage, then
joining in prayer before leaving for the evening performance at
any number of other theatres. Chris Gidney, now director of
Christians in Entertainment, was involved in the formation of
these Bible studies with encouragement from Nigel Goodwin and
Cliff Richard. I was very happy to meet with the group and take
a share in encouraging young Christians in their lives in show
business. There was nothing like this in theatres in the late sixties
and early seventies when I trudged from theatre to theatre looking
for openings to spread the Gospel back stage and front of house.
The Anglican-based Actors Church Union was officially recognized
as having the freedom to visit companies during performances,
and many theatre chaplains provided a helpful ministry, although
not everyone was evangelical so most kept me at arm's length. John
Hester, whom I have already mentioned, was the exception and I
was so grateful for his encouragement.

One morning I walked to Cambridge Circus and stood looking
at the massive frontage of the Palace Theatre. I prayed, as London's
traffic noisily passed to and fro along Shaftesbury Avenue and

Charing Cross Road, 'Lord, if you want me in London's theatres then you are going to have to organize it because I can't.'

I went into the foyer and spoke to a smart uniformed commissionaire. 'Can I see the manager?' I asked. 'You need to go to the stage door, sir,' he replied. So I went round to the small stage-door area and an officious, dapper little man called Charles said, 'You must go round to the front', so I got nowhere. However, I moved along Shaftesbury Avenue to the Saville Theatre and the theatre fireman was acting stage-door keeper. He was pleased to see me, introduced himself as Reg and promptly acquainted me with two other firemen, one of whom asked if I had visited the Palace Theatre. When I told him my attempts had been abortive ,he said, 'Meet me tomorrow, front of house, Palace Theatre, and I'll introduce you.' The next day I was in the manager's office, receiving permission to visit his theatre backstage and front of house whenever I wished.

'I never heard such a thing;' said Charles when I went to the stage door, 'a missionary visiting the theatres.' Gradually I got to know Charles and barriers came down. He had been on the stage in his younger days with Stanley Holloway but never quite made it. His stories were many and interesting, and he gave me a couple of lessons in tap-dancing, not that I needed them but it helped towards good relationships. Very soon I was appointed chaplain to the Theatre Fire Brigade and this gave me permission to visit all the theatres, talk to the fireman and through him meet others in the theatre.

Who could have predicted that one of my first home visits would be to Reg, the fire chief, who became so desperately ill with a chest complaint? He told me that, as a boy, he was a regular at Sunday School, and one of the songs he remembered singing was one about 'a ruler who came to Jesus by night.' Then he said, 'The refrain went like this, "You must be born again".' I sung it to him and he joined in, after which he asked, 'What does it mean to be born again?' Imagine the thrill as I turned to John's gospel chapter 3, and explained how Jesus dealt with Nicodemus. Reg responded as I knelt and prayed with him. Be encouraged, youth leader, Sunday School teacher, and parent; someone had faithfully sown seeds in the mind and heart of young Reg and fruit was borne years later.

I have often found that the more militant the opposition to the Gospel the more that militancy shades an inner restlessness or even a measure of conviction and need. Alf was such an obnoxious individual who almost appeared to have a grudge against life. For some unknown reason he appeared to take an instant dislike to me and made this very clear as we talked at the stage door of the Globe (now the Gielgud Theatre). He loved to 'hold the floor' in front of an audience, and proceeded to ridicule Christianity and tell me plainly what a terrible race of people the Welsh are. He then told me a very smutty joke using characters from the Bible which didn't amuse those present and, least of all, me. I felt I couldn't let him get away with such insults so I quietly said, 'Fancy an intelligent, well-read man such as you stooping to this kind of humour.' He then began to misquote the Bible and joke about hell. I reminded him that the word of God is the truth and is powerful and will not be trifled with. He held out his hand and shook mine firmly as I left and we parted on understanding terms.

Over the succeeding months Alf and I became friends and his attitude changed; his colleagues began to notice his reformed behaviour and were quick to comment. One day when I called, he invited me into his little room. I had given him a copy of the gospel of John and he had been reading it. 'How can I change my life?' he asked. 'I have been a horrible so-and-so and I want to be different.' I turned to his little gospel and we read together some of the life-changing verses from the book he once ridiculed. Alf knelt in prayer and asked God to forgive him his sin. 'I've so much for which to be thankful,' he said, as 'the old Alf' was dealt with in the power of the Holy Spirit.

No book speaks into today's scene like the Bible and it's amazing how quickly this is recognized by the non-Christian public, many of whom have little or no knowledge of its truth. One morning I was standing on the stage in a theatre with a group of backstage staff around me. There were Tony, Alan, Ronnie, Mervyn and, in the stalls, a group of cleaners, all preparing for the evening's performance. The discussions were centred on the things that were happening in the world and in particular the obvious declining moral standards. I took out my Bible and began to read:

> Mark this, there will be terrible times in the last days. People will be lovers of themselves, lovers of money, boastful, proud, abusive, disobedient to their parents, unholy, without love, unforgiving, slanderous, without self-control, brutal, not lovers of good, treacherous, rash, conceited, lovers of pleasure rather than lovers of God.

'Where are you reading from?' someone asked. 'Oh,' I said, 'the Bible'. 'I thought you were reading something from the morning paper, it's so up-to-date,' he said. I closed my Bible and the group went thoughtfully about their duties and the way was open for my next visit.

The Globe Theatre was 'home' to me in those early days. I was always assured of a warm welcome, a cup of tea and, above all, increasing opportunities to get to know the staff. Whenever the L.C.M. publicity department required some updated photographs, the manager and the staff were only too willing to oblige by allowing the use of sets, staff and anything that looked 'theatre'.

Helen Keen had spent her life on the stage and was always ready to be photographed. She had been top of the bill in a number of theatres in the country as well as in the West End and was used to seeing her name in lights. In the forties and fifties she played the lead in shows including *The Merry Widow* and *Lilac Time*. Possessing a fine soprano voice, she was in great demand every

On the stage of the Globe (now Gielgud) Theatre speaking to the staff †

year for principal parts in pantomime. Life, however, became a heavy burden for Helen as audition after audition bore no fruit and management looked for new and younger talent. Helen was forced to seek backstage employment such as dressing the current stars, and it was as a housekeeper that I first became acquainted with her. Her husband was stricken with cancer and she struggled to look after him while holding down morning and evening work. On cue, or so it seemed, I called in the theatre unusually on a Monday morning to find Helen a broken women. 'Hubby's dead,' she blurted out, 'and I'm at rock bottom, I've nothing left to live for!' I listened for a while as she blamed herself and God for her situation and offered what comfort I could. 'Can you meet me in the Mission Hall at lunchtime?' I asked. 'We'll have a snack and a chat.'

She agreed to come and, as I was making a cup of tea. I was aware that she was sobbing in the next room. For a moment I prayed, then made my way to the piano and began to play quietly a song well-known to Helen. I must say the simple melody of 'Love's Old Sweet Song' had me hooked, and I was quite unaware that Helen was moving slowly across the room, first humming then singing the words until she broke into full voice. It was just what she needed to set her off again, to do what she loved most, sing in public. Soon she began rehearsing and accepting concert engagements, and I had the pleasure of playing for her first one in Fulham.

However, there was more to come. One day I called at the theatre and as soon as she answered my knock she said, 'Darling,' (she called everyone darling) 'please introduce me to Jesus.' Helen was on her knees on the hard dressing room floor, I read her through some Scriptures and she asked God to forgive her sin through Jesus Christ. Her Roman Catholic upbringing had given her the knowledge and understanding of Christ's death and resurrection but no personal relationship with Him.

Afterwards we never parted company without kneeling to pray, offering our heartfelt thanks to God, acknowledging our utter dependence on Him and committing our future into His hands. Helen struggled for the remainder of her life, mostly with herself and her relationships with others, desperately wanting to be loved and appreciated and often needing to be reminded of God's love for her. Helen knew of only one way to approach God – on her knees.

As a small boy I was taught to kneel in prayer and during my early days in Anglican circles kneeling was the accepted posture. Scripture lays down no strict rule about the posture we should adopt when we pray. It is possible to pray kneeling, standing, sitting, walking or even lying. I feel that the free churches have, over the years, become too familiar and, as someone has put it, 'too matey with the Almighty'. The nonconformist crouch coupled with the evangelical jargon can be just as much a ritual as that of any other Church with its set prayers, responses and kneeling for prayer. William Hendriksen once said that the slouching position of the body when praying is an abomination to the Lord.

I once made regular visits to the oldest person in the country, a 111-year-old man. The visit always ended with prayer and, although it took an age for him to kneel and even longer to get him up again, he insisted on doing so as no other position was respectful enough in which to approach his God.

King George VI always knelt to pray even when in the privacy of his own room. On one occasion when his valet had an important message to give him he could get no answer to his knock. After a number of attempts to obtain a reply he pushed open the door and, on seeing His Majesty kneeling in prayer, quietly closed it again. When the valet eventually explained, he said he could not interrupt the King's intimate moments with the King of Kings. The King suggested he should have knelt beside him and joined him in prayer. I am also reminded of an occasion when I was leading prayers in a church in Kensington in the presence of Queen Elizabeth the Queen Mother. This gracious lady was the first to kneel as the congregation was called to prayer. There is to come a day when 'at the name of Jesus every knee shall bow ... and every tongue confess that Jesus Christ is Lord' (Phil. 2:10-11).

Within days of leaving the Mission Hall to concentrate on my police and theatre involvement, I introduced a theatre fireman to an elementary Bible Study course called 'Finding Christ'. Imagine my joy when, on visiting Her Majesty's Theatre, I found Gerry answering the set questions from the Bible relating to the magnificent first chapter of John's gospel. Two days later Joan answered the telephone and heard a man's voice saying, 'The Word of God is having its effect.' It was Gerry. 'I just had to tell someone,' he said. When I called to see him, he told me what had happened. He said he had been sitting in the theatre reading his Bible when his eyes fell on John chapter one verses eleven and twelve: 'He (Jesus) came to that which was his own, but his own did not receive him, yet to all who received him, to those who believed in his name, he gave the right to become the children of God.' 'It seemed,' said Gerry, 'as if God was standing right next to me and saying, "I've done all this for you; now it's up to you".' It was at this point Gerry sought God's forgiveness and asked Him to make him a new person. He began to take pride in his appearance; he gave up alcohol and cigarettes, and listened to Christian instruction tapes during his long hours spent on duty. We went together to All Souls Langham Place and he saw the immense value in Christian fellowship. God began to answer his prayers concerning his family and circumstances and, in spite of some setbacks caused through pressure of work which made him struggle, he kept going. Gerry began to find passages in the Bible exciting, particularly the gospels and the Acts, so whenever I made my weekly visit to Her Majesty's he was able to share something new. I shall never forget those times of prayer and fellowship with Gerry, and I recall them each time I pass the theatre in Haymarket.

The well-known actor Alec McCowen happened to visit a Bible bookshop in Norfolk and, while there, purchased a pocket sized King James Version of Mark's gospel, produced by the Scripture Gift Mission. He committed the text to memory and decided to present it as a 'one-man' recital at the West End's Comedy Theatre. I felt it was an opportunity to place God's Word into the hands of the theatre public and visited Alec in his dressing room. For twenty minutes we discussed the Scriptures and I tried to impress upon him the need to apply God's Word to the individual life. He listened as I reminded him of the challenge contained in Mark 10:45: 'The Son of Man has come not to be served but to serve and to give his life as a ransom for many.' He told me he liked the references to children, and I was then able to use the opportunity to explain the simplicity, yet the profundity of the faith of a child as an example of faith in Christ; 'except you become as a little child.' I told him I would pray that God would write on his heart the words he had learned in his head and that he would apply them to his life. Before I left I asked if I might make free copies of the 'script' available to the patrons as they left the theatre. Such a provision had never been known in the West End and I was allowed to take over the foyer bar after each performance. Scripture Gift Mission provided the gospels and Gerry helped me in the distribution. People were invited to come to the bar and help themselves, and over a period of three weeks, in two theatres, 2000 gospels of Mark were taken and a number of conversations were held, and blessing came to many.

I have always been an advocate for leaving the Scriptures with the contacts I have made. The small, attractively presented and aptly named copies of 'Daily Strength', with its verses for each day of the month, are invaluable, as are so many of the fine publications, applicable to any situation, produced by Scripture Gift Mission. They are easily carried around and can be included with letters, cards and other greetings sent by post at little expense. Often where I have failed, the Word of God left in someone's hand has brought life and salvation to a needy person.

Time spent backstage with any individual had to be fairly brief, particularly with a member of the cast. I was always aware that I was there by special permission, because for an artiste to miss a cue was unforgivable and distressing. This necessitated making the best possible use of the time. There was a time when I wouldn't dare knock on the door of a ladies' dressing room, but I ventured to the top floor of the Globe Theatre where a group of actresses were preparing for the evening performance. I knocked and called, 'It's a man, is it alright?' I was told it was and went in to be met by Jenny, in tears. She left home for the show knowing that her marriage was on the point of breaking up. Jenny and I had met before so she felt able to pour out her soul. I listened and, as is often the case, felt helpless, but listening is a ministry in itself, and one ministry followed another and I led her in prayer. There were no instant answers to the problems and she had to go on stage much like Canio the clown in the opera *Pagliacci*, who must go through with his act in spite of a breaking heart. This was the turning point in Jenny's life: she came back to Christ and her marriage remained intact.

'Two people can look at the same thing but will not necessarily see the same thing in the thing they are looking at.' I used this quote by the great preacher W. E. Sangster during a conversation with the likeable Andrew Sachs, star of stage and TV (Manuel in Fawlty Towers). I knew that one of his hobbies was collecting boring postcards so I asked him about it. He immediately produced his most recent additions, the corner of a lounge of a hotel and the corner of a lane in Cornwall on a foggy afternoon. I couldn't drum up the enthusiasm shown by Andrew but commended him for his dedication. 'You know Andy,' I said, quoting Sangster, 'two people will look at Jesus Christ; one will merely see him as a figure in history and at best a good man who commands respect, but another will see him and own him as Lord and Saviour.' I had to leave any follow-up to my friend Timothy Bateson, a fine Christian, who was appearing with Andrew in the same production.

Twenty years visiting backstage areas of London's theatres brought me into contact with a host of famous names, most of whom spoke long enough with me to show just how seriously they took Christian matters. There were some whose Christian faith was real, like Renée Houston, Kathy Staff and Dora Bryan. Memories of Bible studies, organized by Chris Gidney, involving Cliff Richard, Bobby Ball, Michelle Todd, Suzy Brann and others, are vivid, and served as a means of encouraging members of the acting profession in their Christian faith.

Along the way I talked with Sir John Gielgud, William Mervyn, Bill Kerr, Rowan Atkinson, Leslie Phillips, Richard Goolden, Hinge and Bracket, Bruce Forsyth, Linda Bellingham, Terry Scott, June Whitfield, Quentin Crisp (*The Naked Civil Servant*), and Michael Dennison and Dulcie Gray. Others I remember as I see them on TV or, sadly, as I read their obituaries. Contacts, like fame in the profession, were often fleeting, but I can only hope and pray that something said for Christ was good seed and will bear fruit.

When I left West End Theatres in 1988, almost every dressing room in the West End contained a Gideon Bible, thanks again to the help of Christians in Entertainment. It will be impossible to calculate the blessing brought through reading God's infallible Word in the quiet of what might appear to some as being a most unusual place.

Christian Arts throughout the country is stronger than ever through C.I.E. and its indefatigable director, Chris Gidney, who travels the country encouraging artistes and links them up with churches wherever possible.

7

THE CITY OF LONDON POLICE

Since its foundation by David Nasmith in 1835, the London City Mission has influenced the life of our capital city both spiritually and socially; not in ways which always make front-page headlines but quietly and imperceptibly, invariably the result of patient and persistent ministry. It was born in a small cottage on the side of the canal in Hoxton. Subsequently, it had to fight in order to reach and maintain a measure of credibility, particularly in the face of opposition from the mainstream denominations. The Bishop of London even threatened some Anglican clergy with excommunication if they gave the Mission any support.

When I joined the L.C.M., the workforce was divided into three areas of ministry: Mission Halls (now called Christian Centres); Specialist Work (now called Outreach Ministries), that consisted of ministry among railway workers, the fire brigade, the homeless, theatres, police, London Transport, etc; the third area of ministry was centred at some of London's churches.

At the same time as being appointed to theatres and the Mission Hall in Covent Garden, the district secretary, responsible for the oversight of missionaries in North London, suggested that I might consider reopening work among the City of London Police. I had always been interested in the detection of crime and held the police service in high regard. As a boy I had studied the famous criminal cases and remembered details of those involving Jack the Ripper, Dr Crippen, Neville Heath, Joseph Smith, Craig, Bentley and many others. My father was a magistrate for thirty years, my uncle, as I have already said, was Chief of Police for mid-Wales, I played football for the RAF Police in Germany, and incidentally our daughter Marion now also serves as a magistrate.

One morning, while using the L.C.M. Prayer Focus, the day's prayer request was for 'spiritual work among London's police' so I reckoned that with hundreds of people praying that day something must happen. I decided to 'go for it' and made my way to Bishopsgate Police Station opposite Liverpool Street Station. As I entered the front door I made my first mistake, or was it a mistake? I turned left instead of reporting to the reception area. Seated behind a desk in front of me in a small office was Sergeant George Hussey who, when I introduced myself, said, 'I remember the old boy (Mr Thomas) who used to visit us years ago; have you come to do the same work as he did?' 'You've got it right first time, Sergeant.' I replied. George got up out this seat. 'Hang on,' he said, 'I'll go and see the Chief Super.' I'll let former Chief Superintendent Jack Stimson, later to become Commander, give his account of the interview, which he supplied for a police magazine:

George: Guvner, I have a bloke outside who says he is from the City Mission and would like to re-establish the contact the L.C.M. once had with the City Police.

Me: What's he like, George?

George: He seems a decent enough bloke.

Me: I hope he isn't wearing a dog collar.

George: No Guvner, he is dressed like a normal human being.

... at which we both dissolved into laughter. Lionel had to face his appointment board consisting of George and myself. That bloke passed his interview and became a very great asset to the City of London Police. If George and I did nothing else for the force it was the best thing we ever did introducing Lionel to the station and the force. He became identified and involved at every level and we never knew just how much good he did because he would never disclose a confidence.

The interview ended with a caution from the Chief Superintendent, 'No preaching.' I knew what he meant of course and agreed with him. George took me round the station and introduced me saying, 'Look after him, he's one of us.' Both these men were key figures in re-establishing the L.C.M.'s involvement with the police service, and they became my personal friends too. Sadly George died very suddenly*, but Jack Stimson and I are still in touch. Chief Superintendents Alan Francis, Brian Rowland and James Page (who later became Commissioner) also made it easy for me to visit the other divisions, and I thanked God for having opened up the way for opportunities within the force through

---

* George was my initial contact the first day I visited the City Police and, subsequently, I saw him on a regular basis. His wife died comparatively young and I conducted her funeral service after which he gathered his family and friends in his home and requested that I give them a short talk about spiritual matters. One Friday afternoon I spoke to George as he was making his way home in cheerful mood saying he was looking forward to an enjoyable weekend. That night I had a dream in which George featured prominently so on the Monday I went straight to the Federation Office and said I was concerned about his welfare. It was suggested that I go as quickly as possible to Guy's Hospital as he had been suddenly taken ill during the weekend and was now in a critical condition. A young Christian nurse in the intensive care unit showed me to George's bedside and assured me that he would hear me if I spoke to him. I read the Scriptures and prayed slowly and distinctly to him as the nurse held his hand. 'I'm sure he heard every word,' she said. Those were the last words he heard for George died peacefully within the next few minutes.

these sympathetic and understanding men. On my first visit to City Police Headquarters, I met Sergeant Wallace who was seated at the reception desk. When I told him who I was and why I had come he said, 'Thank God, I've been praying for someone like you to visit us ever since I was converted three years ago.' I felt that was God's seal on everything.

The City Police contributed to the happiest twenty years of my time in the L.C.M. This is not to say that the other years were not part of God's purpose for me; they were and I am grateful for them and enjoyed them. I was proud to belong to this elite force with its fine tradition and which, certainly in those days, showed real family spirit. I was treated with respect, never insulted, and even though my message wasn't always accepted, I was given a hearing on most occasions. It was clear to me that the force believed I had a place among them and I was given every opportunity to exercise a practical and spiritual ministry, which, as time went on, led to effective results. I worked closely with the Police Federation and Welfare Department and they, in turn, encouraged me by including me and the family in their Christmas parties and special events. Words of appreciation were plentiful and I often felt totally unworthy of such kind attention. For me to go into one of the stations was to go to a place where friendship was always available.

In those early days all the men had to be at least 5 ft 11 in. tall and this was considered to be short as many were 6 ft 4 in. plus, while the tallest were 6 ft 9 in. and the tallest one of all 6 ft 10 in., and with his helmet he was over seven feet. I told him he could hardly accuse me of ramming religion down his throat. Each City policeman had a prayer on his helmet. The Latin motto for the City of London, *Domine Dirige Nos*, is translated 'O Lord, direct us', and not quite as one copper translated it, 'Gawd 'elp us.' These upholders of the law in the City wore their uniforms with pride and they stood out in any company.

Chatting with City of London Police... †

...and again with a City of London Police Motorcyclist †

Police humour is rather special but City Police humour is unique, and in the early days I had my fair share of 'winding up', but it was never offensive or personally hurtful. Very few people chose to ignore me when I entered their company, and those who did soon realised I was there as a friend with a listening ear and a ready word when required. I sought to ensure that conversations were always natural, and opportunities to share Christian testimony were never ill contrived or open to ridicule. On the other hand I never apologized for the truth, and being the men and women they were, doing the job they were doing, they expected straight answers to straight questions. There were times, so I have been told, when officers would deliberately wait to see how long it took me to guide the conversation in the direction of spiritual themes, and I soon learned that I was expected to say something about God. After all, if the football fan, the cricket fan, the gardener, and the climber have their ready-made topics of conversation and are quick to seek a listener, then why not the Christian?

Before each visit, I made sure I was conversant with current news, be it tragedy or triumph, for I knew those national headlines would be uppermost in their minds. I always felt I had to have answers but when I didn't I had to be honest and say so.

There were times, however, when knowing the answers to somewhat innocuous questions served as an entrance for the Gospel, like the day I visited a group of CID Officers, one of whom asked, 'Who was B. Baring-Gould?' 'Oh', I replied, 'he must have been related to S. Baring-Gould who wrote the hymn 'Onward Christian Soldiers.' One of the officers drew from his drawer a hymnbook, found the hymn and confirmed the information. 'All right,' said a second officer, 'since you're the memory man, who won the FA Cup in 1921?' 'That's easy,' I replied, 'Tottenham Hotspur; they beat Wolverhampton Wanderers 1–0 at Stamford Bridge and the team was – Hunter, Clay, McDonald, Smith, Walters, Grimsdell, Banks, Steel, Cantrell, Bliss and Dimmock, with the last-named scoring the goal.' He believed me and asked how I came by the answer, so I told him that I regularly visited an old Spurs supporter who, every time the conversation turned to football, rattled off the 1921 Cup Final winners. I heard it so many times that I easily remembered it. I then said that I had earned the right to tell them something useful which I had read in my Bible reading that morning: 'God was in Christ reconciling the world unto Himself.' They gave good attention as I explained the verse to them.

This may all sound very easy and plain sailing but for the first couple of years there had been very little spiritual response and I began to wonder where I was failing. I hadn't seen the results I had expected. Was I going about things in the right way? Should I ask the L.C.M. to replace me and move on? Then one day as I sat alone in Bishopsgate Police Station where it all began, I bowed my head in prayer. As I thought and prayed, God seemed to say to me, 'Just stand out of the way and I'll show you what I can do.' It was as simple as that. Lionel Ball was getting in the way, a fault from which most Christian ministers suffer from time to time. I seemed to have a natural gift for making and using opportunities but they were too often spiritually ineffective because God wasn't owning them. It seemed that the light of the Gospel was not being allowed to shine brightly because I was frequently in the way. I resolved there and then to be available to the Holy Spirit and just be an instrument in God's hands. Soon the opportunities increased, more people were asking questions, getting answers and taking literature both for themselves and their families. Committed Christians were joining the force and we set up meetings for fellowship, encouraged by the Christian Police Association with whom I had strong links. Bryan Renno, Roly Tan, John Smith, Peter Martin, Ian Scott, Tony Reed and Reg Wallace were all part of a united Christian presence within the force and gave great support at every opportunity.

'How's the snooker Dave?' I once asked a sergeant. He answered my question, after which I told him that Ray Reardon the former world champion had a favourite verse of Scripture. He was interested and I gave him my Bible asking him to read from Romans 8:18. He did so and read, 'I consider that our present sufferings are not worth comparing with the glory that will be revealed in us.' I explained the verse and its context. He thought for a moment and asked if I would visit his friend, a PC whose wife was desperately ill, and offer him the verse. I wasn't sure what the link was but did as requested that afternoon. I found Alan, but circumstances dictated that it was not convenient to read the verse to him so I went again the following day only to discover that Alan's wife had died. I went to the home, spent time with him and, before I left, asked if I might do as Dave had requested. I read Romans 8:18 and Alan was moved by it, saying that his wife was a Christian and that he longed to know where she was. 'You have given me the answer. She is in heaven, I know it,' he said. We knelt in prayer, after which he said, 'I felt the very presence of God here this morning.' Of course, I had to find Dave and tell him the outcome. Dave was moved but little did he realise that his own young wife was to die soon afterwards.

Being in the right place at the right time is so important as I discovered on a March day in 1973. I had visited Police HQ in Old Jewry and was making my way up Cheapside when there was an explosion ahead of me. Within five minutes there was frantic police activity. My first inclination was to keep away and not indulge in the usual British tendency to be part of a gawping crowd and so hinder rescue services. On the other hand I wanted to be as much help as I could. I went immediately to Snow Hill Police Station and was welcomed by duty officers who told me that a number of people, mostly policemen, had been injured. The IRA had planted a bomb outside the Central Criminal Court, the Old Bailey, and it had exploded causing considerable damage. I saw officers directing traffic and controlling crowds and some of them had torn uniforms and were nursing injuries. In the station I made sandwiches for the extra police personnel recalled for duty before making my way to St Bartholomew's Hospital. I visited twelve officers and a number of civilians. Two policemen were being operated on for serious leg injuries.

I was due to lead an outreach meeting at the centre in Covent Garden that evening, but made alternative arrangements before returning to Bart's Hospital. There I located Diane, the anxious wife of Malcolm, who was in a serious condition in the operating theatre. She was sitting alone and my arrival was opportune. 'I'm so pleased to see you. I've heard about you from Malcolm,' she said. I stayed with her for about three hours and listened and talked as she waited for news. In the locker nearby I found a Gideon Bible (thank God for the Gideons) and began to read from Psalm 23. 'Yea, though I walk through the valley of the shadow of death, I will fear no evil, for you are with me.' 'That's what I need,' said Diane. We prayed and asked that God would be pleased to intervene. We prayed for their two children back at home. Sometime later Diane was to recall that night and relate how she met God in that hospital side room.

Malcolm was too critical to receive any visitors that night but I was allowed in for a brief time next morning and he recognized me. 'I knew you'd be pulling for me,' he said, before drifting into unconsciousness. Malcolm recovered, although his leg was permanently damaged and he was never able to walk the streets as a policeman again.

This, I feel, was a real breakthrough of acceptance as far as my ministry was concerned. Within days I was given a pass enabling me to go on to any police premises including the Old Bailey. When the divisional Chief Superintendent thanked me, I had to say, 'I contributed only a little.' 'Ah,' he said, 'but you were there when needed.'

One of the immense privileges of ministry within the London City Mission is the freedom to be available and to take advantage of being in the right place at the right time.

The Coroners' Court in the City of London is manned daily by a police officer who is responsible for looking after the mortuary and dealing sensitively with bereaved relations of those who have died suddenly through tragedy or heart attacks. Officers are carefully chosen for the job and are on call during out-of-office hours. One afternoon I walked into the office and was told by

David, 'You are an answer to prayer.' David had prayed the night before that someone would show him how to become a Christian. 'What does it mean to be born again?' he asked. There were no telephone calls or other interruptions as I opened up the Scriptures and traced God's way of salvation. Sin, repentance, forgiveness, faith were all dealt with and David's eyes lit up. 'Then,' he said, 'I'm a Christian.' Subsequently David wrote a poem describing his experience. I quote just two verses:

> Lord Jesus, come into my life,
> That I may do your will.
> Help me through all life's troubles,
> That I may love you still.
>
> I thank you Lord for all your gifts
> And what you have in store.
> Lord Jesus, give me all your love,
> I long for nothing more.

Joan and I had dinner with David and his wife Maureen during which I asked Maureen if she shared David's personal relationship with the Lord. She said she did and told us how it happened. 'One day,' she said, 'I seemed to see Jesus in a vision and felt His presence. I could see him on the cross and I asked Him if He loved me. He said He did, and when I enquired how much, I saw His outstretched arms and He seemed to say, "This much".'

I wasn't sure why I was sitting alone in the police dining room at Bishopsgate Police Station one Friday at four o'clock in the afternoon. The early-turn duty had gone home and the day duty and homebeat shift had taken their breaks. The telephone rang but there was no-one to answer it, so I picked it up and the caller asked if Lionel Ball happened to be around. I identified myself and was asked if I was available immediately to go by police car to south-east London. 'Certainly I'm available.' I said. 'One of our retired officers, now a civilian worker at HQ, has gone home and found his wife dead. 'It's not a pretty sight but will you go to be with Peter?' I had known Peter when he was a Met sergeant working at the Old Bailey, and we were on very friendly terms.

With blue lights flashing, we were soon in Eltham. 'I knew you would come.' Peter said, as he embraced me and told me the story. His wife had been depressed and that morning had taken her own life, and the scene that met him on his return home was horrific. For three hours he paced the downstairs while I kept within distance, making cups of tea and listening to his grief. Eventually we sat together and quietly I prayed with him. His relatives arrived and it was time for me to leave. Peter was ever grateful to me and began again to attend his local church. I felt I had done very little but to Peter it was timely.

I have to confess to having to work hard at everything I attempt – nothing ever comes easily to me, not even those things for which I seem to have natural ability. There were still some frustrating early days in the police service where there was a mixture of apathy and scepticism. These constituted very real barriers but ones which I believed could be overcome.

I had the reputation in the early days for getting more policemen on the street than any Home Office directive. All I needed to do was walk into the mess room, approach a table of officers and they would get up and leave. They were safer on the streets than in the hands of the City Missionary. But then it's understandable when you consider I was interrupting their free time and possibly their conversations. The 'old sweats' were much more tolerant than new recruits because they had served in the Forces. They had been used to having a padre around and were quite at home with, as they put it, 'a man of the cloth'.

In one station there was always a 'sergeant's table', just inside the door. One morning I approached it, sat down and all but two immediately left without a word. Peter Emeny (ex-RAF) and Tom Maddison (ex-Royal Marines) apologized to me for the behaviour of the others. These two men made time to stay and talk, and I was ever thankful to them, for it led to a real breakthrough in true relationship-building. Both these fine policemen became firm friends. They opened their hearts to me on matters religious and spiritual, and it led to many years of mutual respect. Peter and I have shared many hours of discussions and a real bond of friendship grew. Our common interest in singing has given us much pleasure, and healthy conversations about the Christian faith have been very productive.

I have to admit to having many acquaintances but very few close friends; Peter is on the list of the latter. Like Tom, who read the Bible I gave him every night, so does Peter. 'The entrance of your words gives light,' says Psalm 119:130 (NKJV).

There is a place for 'blitz' evangelism and, from time to time, 'one-off' contacts demand a clear, concise, no-nonsense presentation of the truth of the Gospel, but the kind of ministry I had among police and theatre personnel required a bridge-building, relationship-building policy. Even so, there have been times when I have used both methods to attract attention and then retain the contact for next time. This requires a natural and relevant approach without being slick. Some people rely heavily on humour and light-hearted quips, but this is not the way to handle serious spiritual questions. Many who know me would be surprised to hear this as I am normally known for my sense of humour, and believe there is a 'time for everything under heaven' (Eccles. 3:1).

I am sure the Lord had a fund of humorous anecdotes. He must have had a twinkle in His eye and His tongue in His cheek on many occasions, but his desire was always to press home a truth to His hearers. 'It is easier for a camel to go through the eye of a needle than for a rich man to enter the kingdom of God' (Matt. 19:24). Can you imagine it? No, of course not; it's almost a joke! Jesus was making the point about the difficulties involved when a rich person is faced with choosing to follow or reject Christ. In John 21 the disciples went fishing at night when they should have been concentrating on obeying Jesus. The narrative says they fished all night and caught nothing even though they were experienced fishermen. As they returned to shore, tired, hungry and generally fed up, Jesus called out, 'Caught any fish lads?' He already knew the answer. You see, that's what happens when you act outside of God's will and do your own thing, especially in evangelism – you catch nothing.

Yet again in Luke 24, two weary people are returning home from Jerusalem to Emmaus, disappointed and feeling let down after the crucifixion of their Master. Again Jesus comes alongside them and asks why they are so miserable. 'Well, because of the things that have happened this weekend in Jerusalem.' Did Jesus have his tongue in cheek when He asked, 'What things?' He knew, of course He did.

Humour is a medicine and we often feel better for a good belly-laugh, but it must be held in context and used sparingly, especially in the cause of Christ. It is merely a tool which has to be used and not abused.

I recall many occasions in the police service when I have been the object of good-humoured banter but have been able to turn it to good account. It was a hot Thursday afternoon and I had been preaching at Tower Hill, so I dropped in at Bishopsgate Police Station and found a group of officers in the resident sergeant's office. No sooner had I sat down when the Chief Superintendent came in, the same one who gave me permission to visit the station and cautioned me not to preach. 'Hello Lionel, what brings you here?, It's not your day today.' 'No,' I said, 'but I know where my friends are and a cup of tea is always welcome.' 'Don't be so sure,' said a PC. 'We can soon put you in Number 3 (cell) and your Governor can't pick locks.' I reached for my Bible and began to read from Acts 16. They listened to the story of Paul and Silas in prison and the Philippian jailer. 'You see,' I said, 'He didn't need to pick any locks, they could have escaped.' They had no answer and the Chief Superintendent was impressed.

I was often mistaken for the Assistant Commissioner who was my look alike. I was regularly saluted and addressed as 'Sir', especially by new recruits. Ernest Bright, in turn, was often mistaken for me. He once got prodded in the stomach and told, 'You're putting on weight.' He took it all in good part and became aware of the confusion caused, and we would chuckle when we met and related our experiences.

The Central Criminal Court, the Old Bailey, has always held considerable fascination for me. Reading accounts of famous trials helped to make me feel I knew the inside of No. 1 Court, although I had never entered it. One day, two of the court officers rectified this and gave me the full treatment, locking me in a Number 1 (cell) and reading the 'charge' against me, namely that I was accused of preaching the Gospel.

The present building with its dome and attendant gold figure holding the scales of justice is a famous London landmark. The inscription above the now rarely-used main door is based on a verse from the Book of Psalms, 'Defend the children of the poor and punish the wrong-doer.'

Speaking one day with a sergeant who was a member of the staff in the Old Bailey, I was asked if I would include the 'sinbin' in my City Police visits. I was only too ready to agree and arranged for an interview with the chief inspector in charge of police personnel.

Frank Jennings had seen active service in desert warfare during the Second World War. His medal ribbons and clasps were visual proof of his service, and he brought some of his attitude and experience to his job. 'You are welcome to try and convert my men', said Frank, 'but start on me first. I'm not afraid of death but

I want to be sure that if there's a place beyond, I shall be there.' As well as being a good talker, Frank was also a good listener, and so I took full advantage of his questions and spent considerable time pointing him to Scripture. Faith played little part in Frank's thinking and, like so many police officers, he wanted to see tangible evidence.

He got his opportunity when I was asked to visit the daughter of a policeman in St Bartholomew's Hospital. Six-year-old Pattie was very ill and the telephone call from her distressed mother Pat at 9 a.m. one day was very brief. 'Please come and pray with Pattie, she has two hours to live and I want you to pray her into heaven.' I hurried to the train, sat in a corner seat and opened my Bible for some word of encouragement. As I turned, unthinkingly, to Mark's gospel, my eyes fell on the words in chapter 5 verse 23. 'My daughter is dying, please come and put your hands on her so that she will be healed and live.' These were the words of another distressed parent spoken directly to Jesus. I pondered this and I questioned, 'Me Lord, going to lay hands on someone who has been given up by the surgeons at Bart's? How can I be so presumptuous? Supposing she dies after all, how do I explain it to the parents?' I was totally unaware that Joan had telephoned a dear friend, Pauline Challender, told her where I was going and asked if she would join her in prayer on the telephone. What was actually prayed in that prayer meeting I am not sure, but I do know that Joan asked the Lord to enable me to do as I was told.

All too soon I was in the children's ward at Bart's, determined to do what I believed was right. The parents and grandparents were around the bed, the curtains were drawn and little Pattie lay ashen white and still. After a brief greeting with the relatives, I knelt at the bedside, placed my hand on the little girl's cold forehead and prayed simply, 'Lord, please give this little girl back to her parents for your dear name's sake, Amen.' The 'Amens' of those around the bed were loud and clear. It seemed as if their faith was greater than mine as Pattie opened her eyes, turned her head and smiled at me. I felt I should leave immediately but spent the day near the hospital checking on Pattie's progress. I returned to the ward and was met by her surgeon who said, 'This is a miracle, that little girl's inside was that of a dead person.'

On the Sunday I took my family to see Pattie and she was out of bed. A week later, as she was being wheeled through the hospital grounds, she said, 'Mummy, I thought I would never see the trees and hear the birds sing again.' The family joined me in Bart's chapel less than ten days later as we held a brief thanksgiving service for Pattie's recovery. Soon she was back at home and attending her local church with her parents.

I have many questions about the ministry of healing, its theology and practice. Why some should be healed and others not is known only to God. Six years later Pauline Challender's husband contracted cancer. He was earnestly prayed for at special meetings as well as by individuals, yet he died, still a young and active man.

Frank Jennings was looking for tangible evidence and I related the story to him. He *was* impressed, but so were many who saw Jesus perform miraculous things yet did not believe. Nicodemus was impressed too and told Jesus so in John 3; he was able to verify that these miracles proved that God had sent Him. Our Lord's answer was, 'Except a man be born again, he cannot see the Kingdom of God.' Faith is the sinner's key to salvation and, once experienced, the result is tangible evidence for the power of God.

Returning to Pattie, I recently decided, after many years of silence, to re-contact the family; so, after tracing them, I telephoned and was delighted to have Pattie answer my call. Peter Emeny has told me that when Pattie was so ill, her father Bob approached him and asked if he would go with him into a church and pray. Neither was used to this kind of activity but the two fathers knelt together and handed the situation to God.

February 28 1975 will be a date etched into the memories of many who had any involvement with the Moorgate Underground train crash. Over forty passengers were killed and many more injured as the rush hour train overran the platform and telescoped.

Young City Police recruit of two weeks, Margaret Liles, was on board the train and became trapped. Less than a week previously I had a long conversation with Margaret, touching on deeper spiritual matters. Imagine my surprise when I rang the City Police offering help and was given Margaret's name as the trapped officer. I immediately went to her address in Wood Green and discovered Margaret's mother had gone to the scene of the crash while her father waited anxiously at home, so I joined him. He was glad of my company. I could only pray for Margaret's safety as well as others still trapped. He switched on the news and within minutes we saw pictures of his daughter being carried out of the situation on a stretcher. 'She's ALIVE!' he cried, and broke down.

Margaret had to have a foot amputated at the scene and was suffering from post-accident and operation trauma. Although visitors were restricted to 'family only', she had asked that I be allowed to see her and at my visit we thanked God together. Just along the corridor was another young woman who had been involved, the daughter-in-law of a clergyman friend. I visited her too but sadly her injuries were fatal and her young husband was left to mourn her loss.

I spent many days visiting police officers for whom the strain of dealing with the bereaved as bodies were identified was proving traumatic. There was no counselling available in those days so I with local clergy did the best we could.

I suppose understandably one of the most thankless jobs is that of a traffic warden. Friends were few on the streets so they were pleased to have the ear of a City Missionary, a sympathetic listener, back in the station.

Helen was a very outspoken cockney, and I mean outspoken. The motorist was by no means always right and Helen would make this abundantly clear. Charlie, her husband, had died suddenly and I was asked if I would conduct the funeral. The arrangements were detailed and clear as only Helen could make them. Charlie would be in the open coffin in the sitting room and would be buried as late in the week and as late in the day as possible. All visitors would be asked to view him, speak to him and shake his hand. The hearse would be horse-drawn, and the undertaker and I would lead the cortège on foot around the square, out on to the main road, then ride the remainder of the journey. Horse-drawn hearses had became somewhat rare in the mid-1980s so it caused a stir even in east London. Our departure from the house coincided with children coming out of school. They were witnessing something for the first time that appeared to have come out of a Dickens' classic, and loving every minute as they called on their friends to join the procession.

We arrived at the cemetery as darkness was falling to find no-one in attendance in the chapel. There were no lights, few hymn-books or prayer books, and the place was covered in dust. I had to conduct the service from memory, give an address and lead the congregation out to the grave, situated, it seemed, among the undergrowth. The committal was duly conducted and the mourners returned to their cars, after which we drove around Charlie's grave with his friends calling out their goodbyes, 'Cheerio Charlie, cheerio mate, see yer Charlie'.

A month later brought a telephone call from Helen. 'I'm diggin' Charlie up; he's not lying there in that derelict graveyard, it's a disgrace. Will you conduct another service?' I agreed to a mini-service, gave a brief address on the truth of the resurrection, emphasising the fact that one day in the future the Lord will return, there will be a resurrection of the dead and all will appear before our Great God. Helen read the words of committal and Charlie was finally laid to rest.

This, however, was not the end. Some weeks later Helen rang informing me that her son, whom she was unable to trace at the time of Charlie's death, had surfaced. Please could I marry him and his fiancée and conduct the wedding *over* Charlie's grave. I'm afraid I drew the line at this and turned down her request, suggesting that this was making a mockery of the sacred rite of marriage. Times have changed, however, and it is now possible to be married in any chosen place.

On another occasion I visited a traffic warden in hospital following an accident in which she was involved. While on duty she was suddenly aware of a car hurtling towards her. The car was obviously out of control and before the warden could get out of the way she had been knocked through a shop window. The only words which came to mind were, 'O Lord, help me.' Miraculously she was not seriously injured. I drew attention to Psalm 50:15 'Call upon me in the day of trouble and I will deliver you and you will glorify me.' 'Write that on one of my get-well cards,' she said, 'and I will show it to all my visitors.' I felt I had to remind her of the last sentence, 'you will glorify me'. God often responds to our cry, but we also have responsibilities to serve and glorify Him in our lives.

I was always deeply indebted to the fellowship of prayer and encouragement given by the committed Christian members of the City Police. There were a number of Christian and God-fearing men and women among both serving officers and civilian employees. There were, however, those with whom I used to meet for Bible study and prayer: Bryan Renno, John Smith, Peter Martin, Roly Tann, Rob Bastaple, Tony Reed and Dave Leach. We would meet to pray almost at the drop of a hat and whenever the need arose. We prayed not only for an effective witness but about the Force as a whole. Forthcoming demonstrations would be covered in prayer, and imminent appointments and replacements which, we believed, needed to be brought to God. We would regularly remember those who were ill or were suffering bereavement. Of course we prayed that men and women would come to know Christ, and our prayers were answered.

8

THE POWER OF THE BIBLE

The Bible has always been at the heart my ministry. Since the L.C.M. was founded in 1835, the London City Missionary was known as 'the man with the Book.' David Nasmith believed the Bible to be God's chief instrument in bringing people of all classes to a saving knowledge of Jesus Christ. The 'Book' was read, quoted, memorised and distributed in homes, workplaces, the open air, on doorsteps, in hospitals, lodging houses and prisons. City Missionaries were concerned for the whole person and were prepared 'by all kinds of means to win some.' They never shirked the opportunity to offer practical help where needed, but at all times this was done with a view to opening up the message of God in a relevant way.

I trace my own interest in the Bible to yet another incident from my childhood. As a small boy I would spend a lot of time with my widowed grandmother who lived in a small cottage on a hill above the small village of New Radnor. My mother would put me on the train at Dolyhir and I would take the short ride to New Radnor where I would be met by 'grandma'. It was considered safe in those days for little boys of seven to travel alone and, if grandma couldn't meet me, I would walk the mile or so through the village and up the road to her cottage. One particular memory of that little cottage stays with me. A large book rested on the table opposite the door. As far as I was concerned it was a Bible (it was, in fact, *The Life of Our Lord*) and I had been told it was a special book. Granddad used to read it so I was told not to touch it, but because I was fond of granddad I wanted to read it too. I spent many hours looking at the pictures but especially at one, a man on a cross with a crown of thorns on his head and blood on his forehead, hands, feet and side. I asked grandma who He was and why He was there; she told me it was Jesus and that He had been crucified for our sin. From then on I never opened the book without turning to the picture. In 1940 I was given my own Bible at Yardro Sunday School and I then could read for myself the accounts of the crucifixion in the gospels. I was fascinated and began to ask questions, some of which my mum was able to answer. My love for the Bible increased and this was encouraged as I attended the Church school at Old Radnor, where a Scripture passage was read each day. I am convinced that the seeds sown in my young mind then were what led to my conversion to Christ and future ministry.

On a number of occasions and as part of my police ministry, I acted as chaplain to parties of widows and mothers whose Royal Ulster Constabulary husbands, daughters and sons had been killed in the conflicts in Northern Ireland. The City Police Federation instigated weekend visits to London as a gesture of support and friendship and to show the bond that exists between the two forces. On one occasion, as I sat at lunch with the City Police Commissioner, we discussed openly the values of the Bible, and to my delight he remarked, 'Lionel, there never will be a book to replace the Bible.' One lady nearby, whose husband and daughter had been murdered by the IRA, said she had begun to read her Bible and had been brought closer to God. The conversation carried on to the day of their departure, and in the airport lounge at Heathrow I listened as another lady showed me a worn Gideon New Testament which had belonged to her son, murdered some months previously. It had been presented to him in school and had been found in his pocket and returned to his mother. 'I now read it every day,' she said, 'and find it such a great help.'

Using the Bible among groups of officers in the canteen came naturally to me. I carried it everywhere and made sure I had one in every jacket so that I was always ready to give a reason for the hope that is in me, as it says in 1 Peter 3:15. There was no embarrassment as I tackled various relevant subjects by referring to scriptures and encouraged my listener to read them there and then. I don't recall anyone who has been converted to Christ through my ministry not having been influenced by something in the Bible.

One day I was asked to go and see Albert, recently retired from the police force but now struck down with incurable cancer and in St Bartholomew's Hospital. Albert was known as a hard, fun-loving, swearing type, who had been a trooper in the Second World War. He had been forewarned of my coming, saw me enter the ward and called out, 'I know who you are, you're the so-and-so sky pilot and your name is Lionel.' He had already been visited by a voluntary worker from the Bible Flower Mission (now London Hospital Ministries and part of the London City Mission) with a lavender bag containing a Bible text. 'Look, darling,' Albert said, 'talk to me as long as you like but not about religion.' In addition a Salvation Army visitor, who had come to 'cheer him up', received even less encouragement when she was seen off with a couple of unprintable words. You see what a challenge confronted me.

I listened to Albert as he took on a serious tone of voice, telling me he didn't expect to come out of hospital: 'I've told my wife to put things right with the bank manager,' he said. 'You know Albert,' I said, 'you're quite right.' Then I paused, put my hand on his arm and said, 'There's a more urgent account to be settled with Almighty God.' Then, remembering what an old city missionary,

Arthur Tarpey, once said, 'Lay up before you're laid out', I read to Albert from Matthew 6: 'Lay not up for yourself treasures on earth but store up for yourself treasures in heaven' and 'Seek first the kingdom of God'. Albert looked silently up to the ceiling. I prayed with him, commending him to God. His words of gratitude were sincere and, when visited by a fellow officer next day, he repeated our conversation. I visited Albert regularly and he actually returned home. Gradually he softened and I am now convinced that he did 'get right with God'. After the funeral an officer came alongside and said, 'Now Albert knows that what you told him is right.'

I couldn't leave this story without a typical City Police sample of humour. The funeral took place on a hot summer's day. There was thunder in the air and, as we all viewed the flowers spread outside the crematorium, a loud clap of thunder was heard. One officer in my hearing said, 'There you are, he's started already and he hasn't been up there five minutes.'

Never underestimate the power of the Word of God in any circumstance, even with those who appear unable to comprehend its truth. I had been called to the bedside of Pat, the wife of a young policeman. She was desperately ill and only able to cope with a short visit. She was a little confused but understood as I quietly read from Isaiah 26:3, 'You will keep him in perfect peace, whose mind is steadfast because he trusts in you.'

I introduced her to Jesus Christ and she responded. After prayer I left her and as Mike her husband showed me to my car, he told me the end was near. 'She will lose her mind, slip into a coma and that will be the end,' he said. Pat died on Christmas Eve and I immediately visited him. My heart went out to him and the two children, eleven and thirteen, but he said this, 'Pat didn't go into a coma, her mind was very clear. Minutes before she died she said, "I'm going to be alright, Mike; I'm going to heaven because I believe in Jesus. You look after the children and we'll meet again one day".' Mike then told me he came simply before God in repentance and faith, experiencing God's perfect peace too. He was then able to break the news to the children.

A visit to a woman in hospital looked as if it could be fruitless when the nurses told me she was 'gone' and was unable to receive any communication. 'Not even her family can get through,' they said. I said to her very gently the Lord's Prayer and she joined in. I then prayed, ending with the Grace – she again joined in and said, 'Amen.' These were the last words she understood.

I have always been an advocate of the use of good, well-presented literature that contains plenty of Scripture verses directly relevant to the situation. There is no substitute for Scripture, which, carefully and prayerfully used, stands alone as the silent means of conveying God's mind to the reader.

In my ministry I have given away hundreds of Bibles and New Testaments to those who have a desire to read God's Word. Next to the Bible and New Testament, I would use the very valuable Scripture Gift Mission booklets, *Daily Strength* and *Words of Comfort*, providing suitable verses for each day of the month. I have given away thousands of these attractive, helpful and popular little evangelistic tools.

With the help of the Gideons, the organization founded to place copies of the Scriptures in hotels, hospitals, schools and other establishments, I was able to present over one hundred New Testaments to the police officers in the section house. Tony Armfield, the sergeant responsible for the section house, gladly allowed the presentation and was given one for his own personal use. Sadly Tony became terminally ill and went into hospital. Mike Sims, the ever-caring Federation secretary, alerted me to the situation, telling me I was the force 'preparer', and he would ensure that the time spent with Tony would not be interrupted by any other visitor so that I had ample time to 'talk', as he put it, 'about serious matters'.

Tony received me warmly and took from his locker the *Words of Comfort* I had previously given him. He began to read the twenty-third Psalm and I joined him. When we had finished he said, 'You know me, I haven't had much time for this kind of thing, but why is this bit from the Bible so popular?' I explained to Tony the very personal nature of the Psalm and that it held the secret of a contented, well-provided, cared-for life in all circumstances. It also provides safety and security in difficulties, particularly in death, culminating in a secure eternal future. Tony thought for a moment, 'Yes, we all need to be ready for the future, but we only think of these things when such as you come on the scene. It's not too late for me to ask for forgiveness is it?' I assured him it wasn't, and together we bowed in God's presence and Tony found forgiveness and assurance in Him.

An old friend and a great influence on my ministry, Gordon Wooderson, used to talk about being 'the fence at the top of the cliff' and he is right. After the funeral some of Tony's colleagues who heard this story, spoke to me and related their Sunday School experiences, quoting John 3:16 from memory. We must never underestimate the power of the Bible to speak in any circumstance. It really is 'as bread cast upon the waters' as Ecclesiastes 11:1 says.

Alex was a fine, well-built police officer, who had achieved success in the world of martial arts. One Wednesday afternoon I stood in Holborn Circus wondering whether or not to go into nearby Snow Hill Police Station. I felt a pressure to go and I am delighted I did, for I found a group of officers having their tea break. This was not unusual in itself but over this cup of tea it seemed like an 'Any Questions' session, first John an avowed atheist, then Jenny, followed by the others. Tea break was up and I lost my congregation but was joined by Alex, who had been hovering. His first words were, 'I'm jealous of you and your faith and have been avoiding you. I can't run away any longer and hoped today I might meet you, but didn't think I would have the opportunity until Friday. I just thought I'd drop in here for a break and here you are. I've had this overwhelming sense of God's presence during the past few days. I had to deal with a drunk in a church and stayed for a while, praying and thinking. Then this morning I read a Bible verse in the daily paper, "Fear not for I have redeemed you, I have called you by name, and you are mine",' he read. It was the best use of a refreshment break Alex had ever made. I read to him John chapter 3 together with other passages relevant to his need. Praying that God would reveal Himself to him, I urged him to think things through, pray and allow the Lord to make him a new creation. I promised to pray for him that evening. I also asked those who attended our church prayer meeting that evening to pray. As we prayed so Alex experienced the New Birth in Christ. On the next occasion we met, he was able to testify not only to me but also to his colleagues, who were utterly amazed at the change in his life and lifestyle.

London City Missionaries have to be ready for anything. I was standing in the lunch queue when a traffic warden approached me and asked me if I would visit her in her home in the Barbican. For a number of years she had received the L.C.M. 'Messenger', delivered monthly by another faithful City Missionary, Maurice Parrington. As I sat in her living room, I listened to her story. Recent sleepless nights had brought what she believed to be demon attacks. She had seen herself entering the next room and carrying her mother under her arm – her mother had been dead several years. She had heard her mother speak to her and felt haunted and frightened by her. There were other strange and terrifying incidents involved which, she thought, would be dealt with by sleeping in the living room. She felt the whole flat was possessed by evil and, in desperation, sought my help. I asked many questions as this kind of situation was not new to me. However, I had no quick answers as I would not claim to comprehend the intricate workings of the mind, the memory or the influences brought to bear by the dead over the living. As always I turned to the Bible and claimed the authority of the mind of God and the ministry of Christ through the Holy Spirit. As I ministered to Elsie the way of salvation in Christ, she began to accept His invitation to repent and trust in His finished work on the cross. I claimed God's promises and authority to cast out all evil and fill the home with His presence, peace and power, committing her to His care and protection.

A young traffic warden at whose wedding I had spoken was always full of questions. Unfortunately she possessed a spirit of discontent and bitterness towards authority (but who doesn't sometimes) and was particularly vindictive towards London's homeless. I was often unaware of the seed being sown in previous conversations, although I suppose it was a matter of routine and just what an evangelist should be doing. Usually the farmer sows seed 'in season' whereas the evangelist is meant to sow seed 'in season and out of season'. One day, as I entered the canteen, I saw Linda sitting alone but she looked different from usual. I remarked on this and she said, eyes shining, 'I have become a Christian.' She told me that recent icy days had forced her to seek warmth in a church. There Linda experienced a different kind of warmth, the warmth of spirit and soul which God's Holy Spirit brings. Her response was to ask the Lord's forgiveness and she gave herself to Him. She said, 'I felt I had become a new person.' 2 Corinthians 5:17 says, 'If anyone is in Christ, he/she is a new creation; old things are passed away, behold all things are become new.' Linda's outward expression that morning reflected her inner experience.

Twenty years with City of London Police can never be erased from the memory. Many friendships were forged and maintained to this day. It was never going to be easy, breaking ground in those early days. Then it wasn't easy for them either because how did they know I wasn't going to 'throw the book at them' and preach a sermon. 'Softly, Softly' or 'Wise as serpents and harmless as doves' had to be the approach, in spite of an initial rebuff or indication that I wasn't really welcome.

The hardest nuts were there to be cracked and I was determined to get to the centre. I acquired a real affection for these men and women and felt I would go to any lengths for them. Like Nehemiah of old, I had a concern for their welfare. Sometimes my ministry to the City Police spilled over into my next appointment. I arrived in my office one day and found on my desk a note to ring Alan who was one of my early contacts in 1969. He could be very brusque and off-hand, but I was determined to win his confidence. In fact, as the years went by, we grew closer and became friends. Now he had retired. I telephoned him and he was obviously distraught and understandably so. 'Pal,' he said, 'I have seen just about everything in thirty years in the police service and coped, but this is too much to bear. I need you.' I recalled what I once said to Alan when he was in one of his truculent moods: 'Alan, one day you may need me and I want to be available.' He then related the sad tragic story of his six-year-old grandson who had been burnt to death in a fire in the flat. I went immediately and had never received a more affectionate welcome. To sit with the family, with a grieving mother, grandparents and brother, was a very solemn privilege. For there to have been bitterness with the grief would have been understandable. They wanted me to read the Scriptures and pray; this was clearly in response to my request. What else is there? Who else is sufficient for these things?

These opportunities only come through building relationships. In a recent conversation with a police officer, he recalled the first time he saw me. It was on the occasion of a muster for duty at a demonstration which was likely to be a bit nasty. 'I remember' he said, 'you came out to our coach and asked if you could pray for our safety. You did so and went to the second coach and did the same. Within minutes we were told to get off the coach, the demonstration had been called off and I turned to my colleague and said, "There you are, that's what happens when you pray".'

I was welcome in the homes of officers of all ranks and almost became a household name. Wives who had never met me would telephone asking for help or thanking me for help given to husbands. Successive Commissioners Sir Arthur Young, James Page, Peter Marshall, Owen Kelly and William Taylor all gave me their utmost support, and I like to feel that I gave them some encouragement in their very responsible position. My post as Missionary Chaplain was confirmed when force orders were reviewed and when I informed Owen Kelly of my impending departure, he wished to be assured that the L.C.M. would provide my successor.

In our home and in a prominent place stands a replica City of London policeman in silver. It was presented to me at a farewell lunch and bears the inscription: 'Lionel Ball City Missionary 1968 to 1988 from your friends the City of London Police'. These are normally reserved for retiring officers who have served for thirty years or more. Some members of the royal family have received them so I'm in elite company.

Only a few months earlier I stood in the Chamberlain's Court at the City's Guildhall and was pronounced a Freeman of the City of London, and once again I have to thank the City Police for putting me up for this honour. During that ancient ceremony within the ornate surroundings of that historic building, I thought briefly of the rural setting of the little cottage on the Welsh border where I once dreamt I would go to London.

My removal to L.C.M. headquarters didn't mean the ties with the City Police were completely severed,

Being made a Freeman of the City of London with Owen Kelly Commissoner of Police †

for it has been my privilege to be called upon to assist in a number of capacities when required, and the police service has treated me almost as a retired officer by keeping in close touch with me.

I handed over to a caring and warm-hearted successor, John Taylor, whose nine years' ministry were greatly appreciated and, I am pleased to say, the L.C.M. still provide the chaplain.

Throughout those twenty-eight years, Joan had worked faithfully and sacrificially in the background, supporting, praying, giving hospitality, homemaking and bringing up our three girls. Often I would be away in other parts of the country representing the L.C.M for two and sometimes three weeks at a time and she would be 'housebound'. Marion, Yvonne and Julia travelled with us to the West End for Sunday services until well into their teens and they too gave their support through music, having themselves made their commitment to Christ. They, in turn, studied and worked hard, married good men and have taken their places in society. Our six grandchildren are a delight and all contribute to being a close family unit.

After working part-time in the UK office of an overseas missionary society, then for three years in the housing department of Haringey Council, Joan realized a lifelong desire to become a teacher. She gained a B.Ed from Middlesex Polytechnic (now University) and taught R.E. (as it was then called) in a large comprehensive school, much of the time as head of department. During my time at headquarters, she also led four fellowship and prayer groups of missionaries' wives on a regular basis and gave them pastoral encouragement and care. As a deacon and weekly daytime Bible Study Group leader in the local church plus being involved in one-to-one counselling situations, her time was fully occupied, and add to this putting up with me!

We thank God for His good hand upon us in the ups and downs of life through more than fifty years of marriage. We are deeply indebted to Him for supplying every need including free holiday accommodation available each year at one of the L.C.M.'s holiday homes and, of course, a house or flat as close as possible to our place of work. In our case there always seemed to be someone who took a personal interest in the family and who often gave the girls those little extras which we couldn't afford.

9

Music Ministry

In his book *The Concise Oxford History of Music* Gerald Abraham
refers to an engraved drawing dating from about 13,500 BC de-
picting a figure, half bison, half man, which appears to be playing a musical instrument. Certainly music of one sort or another
featured at the creation of the world where Job says 'the morning
stars sang together'. Many traits, strains of personality and gifts run
through the genes, we are told, music being one of them.

My grandfather and father were good singers and my brother
a very fine tenor. My sister Noleen and I sang from an early age.
Joan sings, as do our three daughters and our grandchildren. My
grandfather, Lewis Ball, played the concertina, which was easier to
carry around than my piano. Neither my father nor mother played
instruments but encouraged me to play, as we did our daughters
and grandchildren. Not to be outdone, Joan played the cornet in
the Mission brass band as a teenager. Having said this, there is
some music in everyone, but some have little opportunity to show
it apart from being good listeners, appreciators and encouragers
of those of us who endeavour to make music. My parents were
such people even though Dad's patience wore somewhat thin as
I practised on the piano in the room where he was trying to read

the paper. Consequently my piano practice was done at 8 a.m. when he had gone to work. During the second war my parents had saved up and bought the piano second-hand, and at the age of eight I took lessons from Vera Morgan, a local farmer's daughter, each Saturday evening after a bath in the old-fashioned tin bath. When Vera married, I had to then cycle four miles to Evencoed for lessons with another teacher. Eventually I came under tuition from a former concert pianist and for this I was required to do a round trip of twelve miles come hail, rain or sunshine.

Many of my earliest memories were musical ones. I made my 'debut' in public at the Sunday School anniversary at Yardro at the age of five, singing what came to be recognized as the standard one-song repertoire for all beginners 'Jesus loves me'. Of course everyone in the congregation knew it and were ready to act as prompters should there be the slightest hint of stage fright or a lapse in memory. Local singers were heroes to me; Jim Protheroe and John Baynham and, of course, my brother were always worth listening to, as were male voice choirs and quartets. Sometimes Dad would sing to me on request and I would sit on his knee and listen as he sang 'Thora' or 'Don't go down in the mine, Dad', two of my favourites, with 'There's a long, long trail a winding' thrown in as an encore. I was only four when I learned to blow and suck tunes out of a mouth organ and Mum always knew where to find me when she wanted: she just stood and listened for the mouth organ. I would play the Welsh national anthem; I learned it from hearing the crowds sing it the night Tommy Farr lost to Joe Louis in America in a bout for the world heavyweight boxing title. It was said there was a light in every window in Wales at 3 a.m. that day as the patriotic members of the principality listened to the broadcast from America. Dad, to his dying day, maintained 'Tommy won that fight', and not even the official verdict could persuade him otherwise. I earned my first monetary reward at six playing the mouth organ. I would go early to school, call in at the quarry mess-room and play a short repertoire as the workers ate breakfast. My pockets certainly jingled as I ran the remainder of the journey to school. The foreman, however, put a stop to my little earner for he said I was hindering the men when they should have been at work.

When we eventually obtained a radio set, powered by battery and accumulator, programmes were carefully chosen and anything other than what was considered good music was called 'ragtime' and promptly switched off. Not even the resident vocalist on the popular programme I.T.M.A. got a hearing in the Ball household, for those three minutes were a waste of our time. Tommy Handley, the comedian, wasn't, of course.

On Sundays I played and sang hymns, but if we had musical visitors then I was allowed to stay up and secular songs were allowed after midnight – not unlike the devout member of the Wee Frees in the Highlands of Scotland whose Sabbatarian habit was to take down the budgerigar's swing on a Saturday night and replace it on Monday to prevent the bird from enjoying itself on the Lord's Day.

We sang every day in Old Radnor School. Mr Roberts, our head, was a fine baritone and he taught us the old Negro spirituals and some of the patriotic Welsh songs. I did the rounds of the Sunday School anniversaries as my voice developed, and most weeks in the winter Mum would sit me on the carrier of her old bike and take me to sing at concerts as a support item for the local Arrow Vale Male Voice Choir, with my brother in the programme too. I sang in the church choir at Old Radnor and will never forget those singing lessons with farmer Herbert Davies of Hanter. He lived on the hill near Gladestry, and music and singing were next to breathing to him so he loved every opportunity to pass on to others his knowledge. I sang with his daughter Joan and we won the duet for soprano and alto at our first attempt at a local eisteddfod.

I passed the eleven-plus examination and went on to Presteigne Grammar School (now John Beddoes School) where I was a 'splendid pupil' according to my first report, but the standard wasn't maintained.

The seeds of my love for classical music were sown by the head-teacher, W. J. Owen, himself an accomplished pianist, who introduced me to Mozart, Schubert, Haydn and other great composers. He would appear at the classroom door during history, beckon me with his finger, and I would spend the lesson accompanying him on the piano while he played the violin. After that, I played a bit and sang a bit during my RAF days but took no more lessons for either.

When I committed my life to Christ I believed I gave him everything: 'Take my life and let it be consecrated, Lord, to thee', wrote Frances Ridley Havergal, and I made that a serious commitment in words often repeated with very little thought:

> Take my hands and let them move at the impulse of thy love,
> Take my voice and let me sing always, only for my King,
> Take my lips and let them be filled with messages from thee,
> Take myself and I will be ever, only, all for thee.

On my demob from the RAF I joined the Croydon Evangelistic Male Voice Choir, affiliated to the Festivals of Male Voice Praise, and loved to sing the Gospel all over London and the Home Counties. I then became their accompanist and deputy conductor until joining the London City Mission.

Although I began to feel that my days as a singer would soon be numbered and I sang only occasionally, I remembered old John Russell's prayer that God would 'use that voice in his service '. In 1968 I was given the responsibility for leading the London City Mission Male Choir. We sang in the afternoons at the annual meetings each May, and in the evening I would conduct a large mixed choir drawn from mission halls and churches throughout

London. It was a thrilling experience conducting a programme of hymns and anthems in Westminster's Central Hall, particularly on the occasions when we sang choruses from Handel's *Messiah* including the 'Hallelujah Chorus'. Who can fail to understand why, as the great and inspired composer wrote those notes, he said: 'I did think I did see all heaven and the great God himself'?

In the seventies, as a male choir, we recorded hymns for sale as LPs and cassette tapes. Letters came from far and wide, testifying to blessing as people listened to City Missionaries singing from their hearts the praises of God; and the BBC even considered one of our arrangements worthy of a broadcast. Sadly, part-singing among the missionaries went into decline as the older men who could read music retired and with the use of guitars and drums a different style was being catered for. Some of the old hymns gave way to choruses, which suited the growing trend in self-expression and freedom in worship.

The Bible contains divinely inspired songs reflecting many moods and circumstances, and God has been pleased to hear songs of worship and testimony as well as use them to bring many to repentance and to trust in Him as Saviour.

We Welsh love to sing and will do so at the least opportunity, but we do not have the monopoly of the great God-given gift, for there is 'music' in all who will tune in to Him. The psalmist says of such people:

He lifted me out of the slimy pit, out of the mud and mire,
He set my feet on a rock and gave me a firm place to stand,
He put a new song in my mouth, a hymn of praise to our God.

Psalm 40:2-3

Someone has summed it up as 'out of the mire and into the choir'.

Music, among other gifts, is a trusted means of communication. The old minstrels used it to convey news of battles, victories and other events. Lovesick suitors sang to their lady friends, and composers wrote complete works as in opera, relating stories of love and drama. Significantly some of the greatest compositions written by the most famous composers have been based on God or Jesus Christ e.g. Handel's *Messiah*, Haydn's *Creation*, Bach's *Christmas Oratorio* and, of course, Mendelssohn's *Elijah*.

Music and song often crosses barriers and reaches circumstances unreachable by other means. Melodies and harmonies are not subject to class, creed or language, or age or circumstance. Comatose hospital patients have been aroused by the playing of familiar tunes and, in some cases, have literally sat up on hearing tunes such as hymns and Christmas carols. In my own experience a lady whose sister was in a state of dementia and agitation and unable to communicate or be communicated with, could relate to the sound of the L.C.M. male choir on a cassette, mouthed the words being sung and spent her remaining days in peace of mind and heart. A little girl suffering severe pain from cancer could not sleep. Her mother played one of my piano cassettes consisting of sacred music, and the girl was able to lie peacefully and seemed free of pain.

I am in possession of a letter from a friend whose wife was dying of cancer. I had recorded a cassette of familiar tunes especially for her; it was played over and over in her single ward on her final day on earth. My friend told of a prevailing atmosphere of peace and calm as they all sang quietly along with the music. Hospital staff spoke of an 'aura of sanctity being brought to a room of disease'

Another letter from an elderly lady tells of her grief at the loss of her husband. In a state of loneliness and some bitterness she put on a cassette of music old and new, which I had recorded to celebrate fifty years of making music. Among some of the 'oldies' was 'Count your blessings'; the message went straight to her heart and gave her new hope and attitude. If anyone had dared to pass on such advice in ordinary conversation it might have been reluctantly received, but music and associated words can reach into the depths of despair and bitterness. In the words of another hymn:

Down in the human heart crushed by the tempter,
Feelings lie buried that Grace can restore;
Touched by a loving hand, wakened by kindness,
Chords that were broken will vibrate once more.

Music attracts me as nothing else does and I will always stop at the sound of the first note. Like the Welshman who, when visiting London for the first time, saw a sign outside a hairdressers which read 'Haircutting and Singeing'. He was most put out when he discovered there was no male voice choir to serenade him while he was having his hair cut.

As I entered the Globe Theatre one morning, I heard the sound of the piano being played off stage. I could see David, one of the stagehands, peering at a sheet of music and struggling with the notes of a song. For a while he ignored me, then in a sharp tone he said, 'Can you play?' 'A bit.' I replied. 'Then play this for me.' I sat and played at sight the pop song on the music stand. 'Why can't I play like that?' he demanded. I explained a little about lessons, practising and learning notes. 'Can you teach me something now?' he asked. I taught him the lines and spaces on the stave in the right hand and, when we had finished, he asked me if I was a musician. I told him I was but in fact I was in the theatre as a missionary. I used the piano keyboard to illustrate my explanation of the way of salvation: 'Middle C is a good central point at which to start finding your way on the piano.' I told him. 'As in life directions must be observed, without which any would-be pianist is floundering and true harmony cannot be obtained. Equally so, there are directions for all who wish to know harmony with God. Middle C stands for the Cross of Christ upon which he died for our sin, and where we can come in repentance and faith and know forgiveness.'

I love my piano and, next to prayer and the Bible, it is my source of comfort, peace and inspiration. Just to sit and run my fingers over its keys, or to quietly play a hymn tune such as 'Deep Harmony' or a Chopin prelude speaks volumes to my soul.

When my parents scraped together that money to buy me a piano, little did I (or they) think that I would play all over this country, in Germany, the U.S.A., Hawaii, in London's Mansion House and Guildhall, in churches and mission halls and in the open air. 'Take my hands and let them move at the impulse of thy love.' Here I pay tribute to the L.C.M. who encouraged my gift and who supported me in the production of cassettes of piano music, all of which were sold as a Christian testimony as well as to advertise its ministry. 'Take my voice and let me sing' says the hymn of consecration. Christian history bears out the value of the use of solo singing in the work of evangelism, whether we think of Ira D. Sankey, of Sankey and Moody, Gypsy Smith, George Beverly Shea, Cliff Richard, Garth Hewitt or Marilyn Baker, to name but a few.

Playing the organ at the Albert Hall †

Although I had always sung at meetings and services on an irregular basis, the seventies and eighties were years when I, or God rather, rediscovered my gift of singing. Although I had recorded sacred songs, the voice had not reached its full potential until my friend Peter Emeny, a fine bass singer, encouraged me to take singing more seriously and widen my repertoire in order to develop the voice. Around this time I was introduced to Hella Toros, a renowned opera singer, who starred at Covent Garden on a number of occasions. I met her after I had accompanied Helen Keen for a concert in Fulham, when I told her I was a City Missionary. She then asked, 'Does that mean you talk to people about Jesus?' and 'Would you visit me and talk to me about him too?' I said I would be delighted and arranged a date. Hella lived in a large house in Maida Vale, although she occupied just two floors. She took me into her drawing room where, as I expected, stood a piano on which there was a signed photograph of the famous conductor Sir John Barbirolli, with whom she had performed some forty roles at Covent Garden Opera House. Her singing career had come to a premature end when she picked up a germ while on tour and from which she consequently suffered. Hella then formed her own company, specializing in presenting concert performances concentrating on the lives of famous operetta and musical composers.

Before we began to talk about Christianity she offered me a word of caution. 'By the way,' she said, 'if you happen to meet my friend who lives upstairs and she ignores you, please don't be offended. I told her you were coming and she told me she had no desire to meet any miserable Christian who was likely to ram religion down her throat.' I accepted her warning, but I was determined I would meet her friend, look on her as a challenge and prove to her that I was neither miserable nor likely to ram religion down her throat.

Hella and I talked at length about the need to have a personal relationship with Jesus Christ. I used some of the Bible verses she quoted from memory, having learned them from one of her singing teachers who used to read the Bible to her after each lesson. 'I can do all things through Christ who gives me strength' was one of the verses from Philippians. Then there were passages from the Psalms which had also remained in her memory. Her upbringing as a Roman Catholic was in many ways a help, as she was very aware that Christ had died on the cross for sin. There and then Hella went straight to God for forgiveness of sin through Jesus Christ and claimed the word of the Bible as her personal assurance.

I visited Hella on a regular basis and her faith was strengthened as we read the Bible and prayed together. One day she told me she had heard that I could sing and asked me 'When do you sing?' 'Oh,' I replied, 'I sing when asked and sometimes when not asked.' 'Sing for me now,' she requested. Remembering that her friend upstairs, who was reluctant to meet me, was an opera lover, I decided she must be within singing distance. I stood and began to sing:

'Oh how I love him, how I adore him,
my breath, my sunshine, my all in all.
The great Creator became my Saviour
and all God's fullness dwelleth in him',

words written by Booth Clibborn to the well-known tune normally sung to 'O Sole Mio'. I had hardly finished when I was aware of a figure standing at the door and, excusing her interruption, said, 'I recognize the tune but not the words; can you tell me what they mean? ' Over a cup of tea I explained to her how God came down to earth in Jesus Christ and can live in the hearts of those who receive Him. I often visited Marietta and although she never, to my knowledge, responded to the Gospel, she heard it many times after that. To think that at first she didn't wish to meet me.

That drawing room became a place of prayer and witness as well as music. Before I left, there came a ring at the door and in came a tall fine-looking African lady. She held a responsible position in one of the embassies but was very troubled. On hearing who I was and what I did, she unburdened herself, revealing recent years of financial and social difficulties. Beneath all this there lay a great spiritual need and she made this known as she acknowledged that Jesus Christ was most certainly the answer. After listening for a long time without reply, I invited her to bow in prayer. I prayed for her and she prayed for herself and for salvation through Christ.

As I left she said, 'That's the first time for years that I have felt real inner peace and joy.'

On a subsequent visit, Hella asked me if I would consider joining her opera company full-time as a tenor soloist. I thanked her for the compliment but assured her that I was still very much a full-time evangelist and believed I must honour God's call to be a City Missionary. 'Then,' she said, 'will you let me help you to sing for Jesus?' 'But,' I replied, 'singing lessons from such as you are too expensive for me.' 'I'll teach you and all I ask in return is that you teach me the Bible.'

So it was that, in future, Bible studies came first followed by singing lessons. I learned to sing a concert repertoire of popular Italian arias and songs in their original language, carefully watching of course that I was singing morally wholesome words. Invitations came to sing at concerts, some of which I accepted but only on condition that I could include songs of definite Christian content. I was even offered a part in *Don Giovanni* but declined. I enjoyed singing in Italian but this was nothing compared to singing arias like 'If with all your hearts' from Mendelssohn's *Elijah* or 'Comfort ye' and 'Every valley shall be exalted' from Handel's *Messiah*. Then there were the ever-popular 'Holy City', 'The Star of Bethlehem', 'The Lord is my Light', 'How Lovely are Thy Dwellings' and, of course, 'Down from his Glory' to the aforementioned 'O Sole Mio'. Thanks to the L.C.M., some of the last named were recorded and God was pleased to use them as a blessing to those who heard them.

One evening I was booked to speak in Ledbury in the West Midlands on behalf of the London City Mission. I had been asked to sing and obliged with 'Down from His Glory', and as I began to sing, the door opened and a husband and wife walked in. Days later I received a letter from the wife who told me she had seen the meeting advertised, felt she would like to attend but was afraid in case she should be challenged about becoming a Christian. She ran out of excuses for not coming and crept in during the introduction to my song. As I was singing about the Christ who came to earth to save, she came under conviction and there and then yielded to Christ.

On another occasion when representing the L.C.M. at a south coast resort, I had been asked to sing at an evening meeting and I gladly agreed. As I was standing saying good night to folk, a man in his sixties took me on one side and told me how he had spent the last four years after his wife's death looking for God. Somehow he hadn't succeeded until this night when he saw a light in the church hall and came in just before I got up to sing. As I sang, the words went home to his searching heart: 'If with all your hearts ye truly seek me, ye shall ever surely find me, thus saith our God'. 'I found God here tonight,' he said, and, judging by the bright expression on this face, he had, and God had found him.

I have to say to any soloist that you don't have to sing the sacred classics to reach people with the Christian Gospel. Often the simple straightforward hymns sung well will be used by God to touch hearts. 'Come let us sing of a wonderful love' is one of my favourites, or 'My Father watches over me', 'Take my life and let it be' (W. H. Jude) or, one of the Sankey favourites, 'He lifted me'. I was past my middle forties before I agreed to Hella giving me lessons and took it all very seriously. I remembered John Russell's prayer in the field when he asked that God would use that voice in His service. How could I let Him down? I practised every day and memorized all my words so that I could be the best that I could be for God in the ministry of music. The great Irish lyric tenor of the twentieth century, John McCormack, never sang a concert without first spending time in prayer, recognizing that God had given him a unique gift, and asking Him to enable him to use it properly. Isobel Baillie, whose sweet soprano voice enabled her to sing well even in her early eighties, was once asked, after a morning rendition of 'I know that my Redeemer liveth' from

Handel's *Messiah*, what was her secret; she simply replied, 'I know that my Redeemer liveth'.

In the early 1980s I was put in touch with the Hepburn Starey Blind Aid Society, an organization set up to provide Christian influence and leisure for sight-impaired folk. Weekly concerts were held in the New Gallery in Regents Street and professional singers were engaged to provide musical entertainment. Concerts always began with a hymn and a prayer. Eventually I had the responsibility of booking the artistes, and this gave me the opportunity of taking them to a nearby restaurant after the concert for coffee and of course a word of Christian witness. Our patron was Her Majesty Queen Elizabeth the Queen Mother, and Bob Forrester, Mattie Tinley, Eunice Stewart and Mary Miller worked tirelessly behind the scenes, all maintaining the society's Christian foundation. Many fine Christian musicians gave of their talents and through them expressed their Christian convictions.

In many ways my days with the HSBAS served to convince me of the need to have some Christian influence on other organizations and to act as leaven, light and salt. It was a sad day when the society folded due to dwindling numbers, although it had served its purpose and generation more than adequately.

There is going to be a lot of singing in heaven and I intend to get in as much practice down here as I can. On the other hand, practice is hardly a necessity for heaven's choir: everyone will be able to sing, and we'll have new voices and will be singing the new song of the Redeemed in Christ. Will you be among them?

10

L.C.M. HEADQUARTERS

Part of the London City Mission staff member's salary is a free holiday at one of its holiday homes. Over a dozen units have been donated to ensure Mission families can get away and relax. In August 1988 Joan and I were enjoying a fortnight at the holiday home in Keswick, not really thinking much about police and theatre ministry, except for a call regarding a police chief superintendent's wife who had just died of cancer. We were, however, wondering about our future. I felt doubtful about my ten remaining years being spent in the West End and City and half expected the offer of a move to another area of London. When Duncan Whyte, our general secretary, offered me the post of district secretary for North London in succession to Bernard Hooper, it came as a surprise.

The position included responsibility for sixty missionaries working in North London in Christian centres, at churches and in industrial situations (known as specialist ministries). My other hat was labelled deputation secretary for North London within a radius of thirty-five miles. In short, a desk job for the most part. It would be pious of me and untrue to say I spent much time and prayer agonizing over the offer, although of course I did, with Joan, pray about it. I accepted and was sure this was right, even though my daily routine would be quite different. In one sense I was thrown in at the deep end, with my predecessor having been forced to retire early and therefore unable to show me the ropes. On the other hand the very efficient Jean Dyer, who had worked in headquarters for thirty-seven years, was to be my P.A. and she knew the job inside out. Not only was she a fine P.A. but she was a person with great depth of spiritual strength and understanding. Being involved with the day-to-day operational aspects of such a highly esteemed Christian organization brought with it great challenge and no little responsibility. Pastoral care of workers and their families was paramount, and visits to homes and workplaces took me out and about.

I loved my occasional involvement with Tower Hill and Hyde Park open-air teams. I cut my teeth in open-air speaking at Tower Hill when I joined the L.C.M. and stood in fear and trembling on the little platform. In fact I think in those days, I feared the older missionaries more than the hecklers, whose job, it seemed, was to put us younger ones right theologically. Open-air work has changed; you will no longer encounter the large crowds and hear furious debate between speaker and heckler, and fewer people actually listen, but I am convinced that more personal conversations take place than in those days. London City Missionaries seemed to own Tower Hill at 12.30 p.m. on a Thursday and Hyde Park on a Friday at 6 p.m., not forgetting Woolwich Square, also on a Thursday. They took on all-comers and made little of many of their arguments with their knowledge of the Scriptures. They would be in their element on the annual visit to Epsom racecourse on Derby and Oaks days where we would visit caravans in the morning and preach between races in the afternoon. Imagine the twinkle in our eyes when, after the Derby, we would sing 'Oh Happy Day that fixed my choice'.

An important aspect of my job at HQ was involvement with the movement and placing of staff, and this meant that the course of the lives of missionaries and their families could be changed. Knowing God's will for your own life is often difficult enough but when you are seeking God's will on behalf of other people's next step, then it is almost frightening to contemplate.

Halfway through my time in the so-called corridors of power, the L.C.M. moved from regional management to functional management, and George Hider, a respected colleague, and I were appointed directors. He became director of Christian Centres and I became Specialist Ministries' director. My heart, however, remained in evangelism and some even questioned my leaving the field of ministry to become desk-bound, but I felt it was right that I should be able to pass on the benefit of experience gained in actual evangelism, even though there were some unhappy moments. Leadership inevitably has its difficulties and even in Christian organizations life can sometimes be anything but smooth because teams consist of individuals, and individuals, naturally, sometimes want their own way.

I learned much about the ministry of the London City Mission from reading its history and knowing many of its workers. In 1835 its founder, David Nasmith, and his colleagues pledged themselves to take the Good News of Jesus Christ to the capital's people, and their successors have never deviated from the original conviction. The Mission's influence in London's life as contained in its fine archive of resource material was preserved through fire and water in two world wars, and this in spite of being bombed out of our headquarters in the City during the height of the 1940 blitz. Its strength lay in the power of God's Holy Spirit and its adherence to the Gospel that changes lives and brings people from 'darkness to light and from the power of Satan to God'. Add to this the praying, financial and practical support of Christians throughout the country.

Joan and I are now living in retirement in Herne Bay. God, as He always does, has provided for us, through a generous Mission supporter, retirement accommodation offered to us by the L.C.M. just as we were coming to the close of our service – such perfect timing. We are involved in evangelism down here in Kent and one day, as part of a small outreach team, we were singing carols in a pub on the seafront. Speaking with the landlady she said she was impressed that we should pay them a visit. 'You see,' she said, 'as a girl my happiest days were linked with my involvement in a London City Mission Hall in south east London.'

My story is almost told except for the fact that I had almost finished the draft when news came through that my mother had died in hospital in the small Hereford town of Leominster. For five years following the death of my father she lived alone in the little cottage in Dolyhir, determined to make the best of life after giving Dad loving care in his frailty and, I'm convinced, keeping him alive until he was taken into hospital for the last seventy-two hours of life..

In spite of breaking her wrist and hip on separate occasions, her fight to live remained. Whenever I visited her, we would pray and read together from the Bible. How she loved the twenty-third psalm. Her last three years were spent in residential care before a fall took her into hospital and old age plus an infection overcame her remarkable strength; she slipped away into heaven one Sunday evening just as one of her favourite TV programmes, *Songs of Praise*, was being broadcast.

Joan and I went to the little chapel of rest where she lay in the open coffin, her unlined face looking peaceful and dignified, with the slight expression of determination she showed in life. Somehow we didn't feel we were in the presence of death; we talked together as if she was the silent listener to our conversation and as we bowed together in prayer, we gave thanks to God for her life and Christian witness. As we kissed her forehead we didn't say 'goodbye' just 'farewell until we meet again'.

The same day we were able to make a last nostalgic visit to Blacklands. It was a dark damp day, but what we saw wouldn't have been any more pleasing to heart and eye if we had done so on a bright summer's day, such as I remember fifty years before. The once well-kept low hedge was overgrowing the little pathway leading to the front door and the little garden area was full of weeds. The neat little frontage opposite the cottage door looked unkept and the windows curtainless and grimy. We stood silent and sad at heart, reflecting on what used to be; then I recalled Fredrick O'Connor's famous poem – 'The Old House' and recited it as fitting our situation:

Lonely I wander through scenes of my childhood,
They call back to memory the happy days of yore,
Gone are the old folks, the house stands deserted,
No light in the window, no welcome at the door.

Here's where the children played games in the meadow,
Here's where they sailed their wee boats on the burn,
Where are they now? Some are dead, some have wandered,
No more to their home will those children return.

Lonely the house now and lonely the moorland,
The children are scattered, the old folks are gone,
Why stand I here like a ghost and a shadow,
'Tis time I were moving, 'tis time I moved on.

We drove through the little hamlet where Mum lived as a child, and saw along the rough track the small building, once a cottage now a farm outhouse, where she was born more than ninety years ago. Then on we went and saw the little school where Dad learned the three Rs and which he left at the age of twelve to work on a farm. Strangely we felt part of an era which existed before we were born.

The funeral, well a thanksgiving service really, was an occasion when close on a hundred friends and acquaintances from near and far joined the family to sing Mum's favourite hymns and remember her with gratitude. I was privileged to accompany one of her favourites 'Guide me, O thou great Redeemer', on the lovely organ which, fifty years ago, she would pump as I practised, before electricity did the job for me. In my address I referred to her sense of family values, her sense of fun and her faith; then came these words which I penned as I quietly sat in preparation less than two hours before:

> We loved so much about her life,
> Her fun, her faith, her care,
> We'd never want for anything
> When Nanny Ball was there,
> And even though she's left us,
> We sorrow not as some,
> She gave us so much loveliness
> Thank God – Thy will be done

Somehow the closing hymn, 'God be with you till we meet again', didn't sound like the dirge it often does; it was as if she was singing it too. As we followed her coffin through the church door, we were to pass the spot where my brother's ashes lay and we remembered him and his velvet tenor tones which were silenced at the age of fifty-four. Then she was laid to rest with Dad and among her friends in the little graveyard across the road, less than a hundred yards from the school where she cooked for children in the 'sixties and 'seventies, prior to its closure. And so we bade farewell to a remarkable lady who taught us the good things in life, to play a positive, constructive role in society, to pray, worship God and read the Bible.

Well, the book is almost written but not the story, for the word 'retirement', we are told, shouldn't apply where Christians are concerned as all are required to be the Lord's ambassadors wherever we are. Each day Joan and I commit ourselves to the Lord for His use, in the knowledge that one of the abilities He requires is availability. We feel we must, if at all possible, meet the people of our locality and try to bring Christian influence into every situation on the principle of 'salt and light'. We have joined the horticultural society, attend the village church, lead a prayer group and 'bloom where we're planted', an instruction which came from the Scriptures within a year of our arrival in Herne Bay. Joan goes to the Women's Institute, attends a painting class and helps with the local toddlers' group. I have joined the Historical Records Society, speak at various kinds of meetings, preach at local churches, served as their president for three years, write a regular 'thought for the week' for the Herne Bay Times, play the piano as a 'way in' for the Gospel, and seek to use every opportunity to share Christ with others. Our beloved London City Mission isn't forgotten, for Joan is now the Herne Bay support secretary.

I used the word 'availability' earlier. Well, one day I took Joan and our granddaughters to the swimming pool, but because I was dressed in my gardening clothes I felt slightly conspicuous. On making my way back to the car I happened to see a Union flag-draped coffin on a hearse outside the parish church. Standing nearby, I could see the vicar dressed in cassock and surplice and waving in my direction. As I approached he said, 'I've got a funeral in two minutes and the organist hasn't turned up.' I knew what he was asking so offered my services, but he thought I wasn't 'properly dressed' so he hesitated. I thought, take me as I am or do without an organist. I went and found Joan and told her, 'I'll see you in half an hour, I've got a funeral', and hurried up the side aisle of the church towards the organ. Remembering Walford Davies's 'Solemn Melody', I played the coffin in, accompanied two hymns, saw the cortège out with Handel's *Largo*, switched off the organ, put on my jumper and made my way to the car without so much as a word from anyone. A friend rang me some days later and told me that a friend of his attended a funeral recently and some scruffy chap came in as if from the street and played the organ. Don't shoot the organist, you may need him.

Opportunities to share the Christian faith are in abundance as with the gas man who told me he had some good news for me and, after listening to him, I informed him that I had some even better news for him, news that is of utmost eternal value, and quoted John 3:16; he promised to give it serious thought. Then there was the neighbour who was making early preparations for his and his wife's funerals and wished to borrow a hymn book. We sat for an hour in our garden as I showed him how to prepare himself spiritually for that day, and gave him Michael Green's helpful book, *My God*.

Joan and I have recently celebrated fifty years of marriage when we enjoyed gathering with family and friends. It was with certain pride and much gratitude to God that we looked at our three gifted daughters – Marion, Yvonne and Julia, their fine husbands, David, Christopher and Terry and six delightful grandchildren, William, Guy, Emily, Hannah, Lewis and Eliza – two in each family. We thank God that he has placed his hand upon all of them.

With the Ball Family

ACKNOWLEDGEMENTS

Given the opportunity, we should all acknowledge in some way the debt we owe to those who, over the years, have played a part in the development of our character. Many of those who were such a help to me are no longer with us but have been mentioned already. Some, due to their unique character, come close to being irreplaceable, like my dear friend Kinsey Croose, a Welsh farmer, whom I knew almost a long as I can remember. Although considerably older than me, we had an affinity in spiritual, musical, historical and poetical matters, as well as things humorous, particularly relating to the locality. A godly, good, gracious, honest and humble man, he said to me soon after I joined the L.C.M., 'As a preacher you are in the greatest calling of all.'

There are host of others who deserve to be acknowledged such as any RAF pals with whom, through my own fault, I have lost touch; may this book be the means of some reunions. And what about all the City Missionaries, past and present, with whom I served and who were often just the inspiration I needed, as well as the occasional source of timely rebuke? I think, too, of some who recognized in me leadership gifts and were prepared to trust me, like Duncan Whyte, the L.C.M.'s general secretary, whose wise counsel and encouragement have meant so much. I esteem him highly as a theologian, thinker and inspiring preacher.

Then there is Sandy Millar who kindly provided the Foreword to this book, and Nicholas Rivett-Carnac, two men of God who were such a blessing as we worked together in the seventies. I mustn't forget the many prayer partners who prayed, often when I forgot to pray for myself, particularly when things were tough, and who seemed to know just when to stand by me. I think, too, of congregations of Christians of all denominations who were kind enough to let me speak to them and, in particular, the fellowship at Eldon Road Baptist Church, Wood Green, where Joan and I were involved for more than thirty years, made many friends and had the privilege of serving in a number of capacities.

Finally, and most importantly, I am bound to pay tribute to my immediate family. Joan, Marion, Yvonne and Julia who gave me to God and to others, even when they needed me most, and how the pangs of regret still return to haunt me, especially when I recall those long periods away from home promoting the work of the London City Mission. So much responsibility fell on Joan during the early and formative years in the girls' lives, and the fact that they have done so well in life is, in large measure, down to her.

In 1991 I was taken seriously ill with an acute prostate problem (that which is common to man) and was rushed into hospital from my doctor's surgery, as there was no time to go back home first. I was 'patched up' behind a screen in the corridor and assigned to a ward. Then, the following day, I was given special permission to conduct a marriage blessing service for a young police couple before returning to the hospital. The pain, however, was excruciating and a surgeon was sent for, who arranged a biopsy followed by an emergency operation as there was concern at the discovery of a growth. The shrewd knowledge and skill of this man was timely and, with the prayers of Joan and the family, saw me through a situation about which I knew very little. There was further cause for concern when it was discovered that there was more paraprotein in my blood than was good for me and my E.S.R. (Erythrocyte Sedimentation Rate) was sky-high. However, many people were praying and the prognosis was more encouraging. Duncan Whyte, our general secretary, felt led to lay hands on me at a senior staff conference, from which time each visit to the specialist brought me better news. Now I am told things are back to normal and I praise God for His goodness as well as for the support of a loving, united family.

Having now read the book, you will in no way be persuaded into thinking that my life and ministry has been one continual round of high spots and successes. I made many mistakes and let the Lord and my fellow human beings down, and there were things done and undone. I must have offended many people and for this I ask forgiveness, and there were times when selfish pride took first place. God, I know, was patient with me as were many to whom I ministered and with whom I worked, but in all this He was able to do something with an ordinary country lad and, in a small way, use him to be a blessing to others. My prayer is that this book should bring glory to God and that some should be encouraged while others should consider Christ, repent of sin, and trust Him for salvation, for He alone is 'the TRUE and LIVING WAY'. To God be all the glory.

Christian Focus Publications
publishes books for all ages

Our mission statement –

STAYING FAITHFUL
In dependence upon God we seek to help make His infallible Word, the Bible, relevant. Our aim is to ensure that the Lord Jesus Christ is presented as the only hope to obtain forgiveness of sin, live a useful life and look forward to heaven with Him.

REACHING OUT
Christ's last command requires us to reach out to our world with His gospel. We seek to help fulfil that by publishing books that point people towards Jesus and help them develop a Christ-like maturity. We aim to equip all levels of readers for life, work, ministry and mission.

Books in our adult range are published in three imprints.
Christian Focus contains popular works including biographies, commentaries, basic doctrine and Christian living. Our children's books are also published in this imprint.
Mentor focuses on books written at a level suitable for Bible College and seminary students, pastors, and other serious readers. The imprint includes commentaries, doctrinal studies, examination of current issues and church history.
Christian Heritage contains classic writings from the past.

Christian Focus Publications Ltd
Geanies House, Fearn,
Ross-shire, IV20 1TW, Scotland, United Kingdom
info@christianfocus.com

Our titles are available from quality bookstores and
www.christianfocus.com